REVERDY C. RANSOM

Black Advocate
of the
Social Gospel

Calvin S. Morris

UNIVERSITY
PRESS OF
AMERICA

Lanham • New York • London

Copyright © 1990 by
University Press of America®, Inc.
4720 Boston Way
Lanham, Maryland 20706

3 Henrietta Street
London WC2E 8LU England

Library of Congress Cataloging-in-Publication Data

Morris, Calvin S. (Calvin Sylvester), 1941–
Reverdy C. Ransom : Black advocate of the social gospel / by
Calvin S. Morris.
p.   cm.
Includes bibliographical references.
1. Ransom, Reverdy C. (Reverdy Cassius), 1861–1959.   2. African
Methodist Episcopal Church—Bishops—Biography.   3. Methodist
Church—United States—Bishops—Biography.   4. Social gospel.
5. United States—Race relations.   6. Race relations—Religious
aspects—Christianity—History of doctrines—19th century.   7. Race
relations—Religious aspects—Christianity—History of doctrines—20th
century.   I. Title.
BX8449.R35M67   1990   287'.8'092—dc20   90–31217 CIP
[B]

ISBN 0–8191–7766–0 (alk. paper)
ISBN 0–8191–7767–9 (pbk. : alk. paper)

The paper used in this publication meets the minimum requirements of
American National Standard for Information Sciences—Permanence
of Paper for Printed Library Materials, ANSI Z39.48–1984.

This work is lovingly and gratefully
dedicated to

the memory of my grandmother, Ida Lydia Morris, my
mother Dorothy Lee Morris and my mentors and
friends, Mr. Alphonso & Mrs. Lottie
"Sister" Wilson, Mr. Matthew
McIntyre, the Reverend
Samuel Govan Stevens
and the Reverend Dr.
Harrell F. Beck

ACKNOWLEDGEMENTS

Many persons have contributed to the successful completion of this study. I regret that I cannot thank all of them at this time. I must express my appreciation to the librarians and staffs of Moorland-Spingarn Research Center, Howard University; Wilberforce University; Payne Theological Seminary; the Schomburg Research Center; and the Howard University Divinity School for their kind aid and assistance. Special thanks goes to Dr. Lawrence N. Jones, Dean, Howard University School of Divinity, who brought to my attention the subject of this study and who received my repeated queries with genuine interest and concern. He travelled with me on this journey and I am grateful for his presence and encouragement. My thanks goes also to the Administrative Assistant in the office where I am privileged to work. Mrs. Benittia Jones is a trusted colleague and friend on whom I can depend in all seasons.

I am also grateful to my colleagues Drs. David Hall, John Cartwright, Howard Zinn, Roy Glasgow and Joseph Boskin for their advice, counsel and support. I am particularly indebted to Joseph Boskin my mentor and guide over the years.

There are also friends and loved ones to be remembered, without whose love and care I could not have survived: my father, and step-mother; Abner & Lucinda Williams; Willie Barrow; Albert Naples, Jr.; Paul and Harriet Keyser; Charles and Shirley Coverdale; Larry and Maxine Edmonds; my college professor and advisor Richard C. Winchester and his wife Connie; and my beloved daughters, Dorothy Rebecca and Rachel Elaine Morris.

TABLE OF CONTENTS

REVERDY C. RANSOM
Editor A. M. E. Review

The powerful leaders of the religious sects (who came closer to the mass of the Negro people than the better-known writers and intellectuals) are only shadowy figures. We don't know much about them and probably never will.[1]

Until recently the lives and careers of outstanding black clergymen, the undisputed leaders of the late nineteenth and early twentieth century black community, were all but ignored, or considered inaccessible to American historical scholarship and research. Fortunately, historical astigmatism of this kind has been partially corrected. Studies of black religious luminaries such as Edward Wilmot Blyden, Henry McNeal Turner, Daniel Alexander Payne and Francis J. Grimke are welcomed additions to an expanding body of historical knowledge.[2] This dissertation therefore attempts to add to that corpus of historical knowledge by studying the life and Social Gospel ministries of Reverdy Cassius Ransom, a leading African Methodist Episcopal churchman. Historian, Carter G. Woodson in <u>The History of the Negro Church</u>, describes Ransom as a Social Gospel trailblazer among black clergymen of his day.[3] This study does not attempt to cover his long and eventful life (1861-1959), but addresses his life and career prior to his elevation to the episcopacy of the African Methodist Episcopal Church (1924). However, data relating to his ministry and involvement after 1924 will be included when pertinent.

Although Ransom was a major figure in the American racial and religious arena for more than half a century, he has gained only cursory historical mention.[4] As a result, while aspects of Ransom's life and thought have been addressed,[5] to date, a study of his life has not been completed.[6] Thus, the primary purpose of this work is to increase and deepen the understanding of American racial history as reflected in the life and ministry of Ransom, who was a member of its largest minority group.

The over-riding fact of race which was so large an element in restricting the access of minority persons to activities outside their own communities dictated that Ransom's life as a minister would be directed toward the elevation and advancement of black people. Specifically, Ransom sought racial advancement from the standpoint of black Christian activist and Social Gospeler. He perceived the most elemental precepts of Christianity to be the Fatherhood of God and the Brotherhood of man, and this became the point and the horizon of his religious and racial vision. While the racial and thus, social turmoil of Ransom's era asserted an evolutionary inferiority to black people, Ransom attempted to counter the violent racist climate with religious precepts and an awareness that was firmly

2

rooted in the racial and religious experience of black people. He believed that black people's right to liberty and justice in America was part of God's evolving purpose and that equal rights were inherent in the country's democratic tradition and creed. In Ransom's opinion, American Blacks had a specific destiny and responsibility to strive to manifest God's kingdom on earth. The inherent religious ideal in Ransom's perception was that Christian Americans would become the embodiment of God's will in a world free of racial and social injustice.

Ransom repeatedly asserted that America's right to spiritual distinction would depend upon its treatment of black people. In his view, the validity of the Christianity and democracy expounded by white America was tied to the Whites' response to the issue of race. He wrote that "The practical application of Christianity meets a real test every time it is confronted by an American Negro. The Negro is a standing challenge to the earnestness of its faith..."[7]

In 1903, W.E.B. DuBois stated that the A.M.E. Church was "probably...the greatest voluntary organization of Negroes in the world."[8] Ransom's church career was centered in this broad-based structure. He utilized the power of the A.M.E. denomination in order to pursue his racial and social objectives. However, it is significant to note that although the church was Ransom's organizational base, he did not always strictly adhere to its ecclesiastical directives.

Ransom began his ministerial career as a student in 1884 at the age of twenty-three. At that time, the black church was the most powerful and influential institution in the black community and acted, as Albert J. Raboteau has written, as "an agency of social control, a source of economic cooperation, an arena for political activity, a sponsor of education, and a refuge in a hostile white world..."[9] The church was the primary vehicle of racial self-help and solidarity within the black community. Both W.E.B. DuBois and Ransom were aware of the church's unique position and each perceived it as the "social center" of black life and the foundation upon which Afro-American culture was built.[10]

Ransom was convinced early that if the church was

to maintain its preeminent position in the community, it must respond to the demands of twentieth century American life. This perspective was reinforced by the societal changes he witnessed while pastoring in Springfield and Cleveland, Ohio, Chicago, Boston and New York between 1890 and 1912. While seeking to address problems which arose from the large migration of rural southern Blacks to northern urban centers, Ransom recognized the inadequacy of traditional church structures to minister to this new population. Thus, although committed without serious reservation to the church, Ransom was not uncritical of the church's shortcomings in the area of social welfare. For Ransom, it seemed that the structures of the church were ill-prepared to respond to those social needs, and he therefore created adjunct institutions which were more consistent with his definition and vision of a socially relevant church.

The Social Gospel Movement was enormously important in the development of Ransom's ministerial philosophy and style. The height of this religious crusade occurred during the years of 1890-1914. The movement addressed itself from a theological viewpoint to the issues of employment, housing health care, education and political reform.

Church Historian, Robert T. Handy has described Social Gospelers and their cause as

> .....the movement among liberal-minded Protestant evangelicals to rally Christian forces to deal with the problems of society which were intensifying in the late nineteenth and early twentieth centuries... The difficulties arising out of industrialization and urbanization were their particular concern. They sought to parallel the Protestant emphasis on the individual and his freedom with attention to social realities, especially those of the urban slums and of the condition of labor.[11]

Similarly, Ransom believed that the church, in order to minister to human need, had to be concerned about every area of people's existence, whether social, political, industrial or cultural. Thus, he fought for adequate wages for working people; educational opportunities for the poor; the right of Blacks to vote;

4

as well as better housing and working conditions for the poor and working classes. Ransom came to exemplify in his ministry the clergyman as social and political activist in a manner that was consistent with his image of the church.

During his childhood and youth, the black church attracted many leaders who were similar activists and role models for Ransom's developing religious consciousness. C. Vann Woodward has called such men "shadowy figures" and "powerful leaders (who came closer to the mass of the Negro people than the better-known writers and intellectuals)."[12] The leaders to whom Woodward refers are such A.M.E. clergymen as Daniel Payne, Benjamin Arnett, and Henry McNeal Turner. Those ministers, along with numerous others, exercised, in addition to their ecclesiastical powers, enormous influence as politicians, diplomats, educators, and authors. They were the leaders of the black community before 1900,[13] and W.E.B. DuBois described their preeminence in this manner: "The preacher is the most unique personality developed by the Negro on American soil. A leader, a politician, an orator, a boss, an intriguer, an idealist - all this he is ....."[14]

Like his contemporaries who have been identified, Ransom was a leader and minister who became a significant figure within the larger black community. His importance can be measured in part by the assessment given of him by his contemporaries after his death. A fellow A.M.E. Bishop, D. Ward Nichols, a colleague of Ransom, described him as one of the "leading lights"[15] not only of the A.M.E. Church, but also of the national and international community. Another A.M.E. contemporary, the Reverend Richard Allen Hildebrand, in recalling Ransom's pastorate at Bethel A.M.E. in New York, characterized Ransom as "one of the stalwarts of social and religious justice."[16] William H. Ferris, a highly distinguished scholar, respected critic and editor,[17] declared Ransom to have been one of the most "gifted" orators of his time.[18] Many of Ransom's numerous addresses and sermons were published by popular demand and are listed in various publications which highlighted black oratorical excellence.[19] A poet and author, Ransom wrote six books[20] (including his autobiography) and numerous poems and articles for secular as well as religious newspapers and magazines.

The development of Ransom's life and activity must

5

be investigated. He was born and reared in the midst of both poverty and racial proscription, yet he became an outspoken statesman for racial and social justice. Any contradictions in Ransom's philosophy and life can be explained only with an exploration into his character, the people, and the times from which he emerges. While still a young man in Ohio (during the 1870's) Ransom was keenly aware of the deteriorating position of Blacks in America, and as a recent graduate of Wilberforce University, he began in the late 1880's and the early 1890's, along with other black leaders, to fashion a strategy for race survival and growth. However, Ransom responded to the basic question with which numerous other black leaders were struggling in a unique manner. Often, his response was as varied and as complex as his times, and a close look at Ransom's life reveals that a study of this nature is nor only historically justified, but long overdue.

Footnotes

[1]C. Vann Woodward, "The Negro in American Life: 1865-1918," Interpreting American History: Conversations with Historians, Part II, p. 56.

[2]Hollis R. Lynch, Edward Wilmot Blyden: Pan-Negro Patriot, 1832-1912 (New York: Oxford University Press, 1967); Edwin S. Redkey, Black Exodus: Black Nationalist and Back-to-Africa Movements, 1890-1910 (New Haven: Yale University Press, 1969); Gayraud Wilmore, Black Religion and Black Radicalism (New York: Anchor Books, 1973); Charles Dunmore Killian, "Bishop Daniel A. Payne: Black Spokesman for Reform" (Ph.D. dissertation, Indiana University, 1971); Arthur Paul Stokes, "Daniel Alexander Payne: Churchman and Educator (Ph.D. dissertation, Ohio State University, 1973); David Wills, "Aspects of Social Thought in the African Methodist Church, 1884-1910 (Ph.D. dissertation, Harvard University, 1975); and "The Meaning of Racial Justice and the Limits of American Liberalism, "The Journal of Religious Ethics, 6/2 (Fall 1978), 199-215; Henry Justin Ferry, "Francis J. Grimke: Portrait of a Black Puritan" (Ph.D. dissertation, Yale University, 1970).

[3]Carter G. Woodson, The History of the Negro Church (Washington, D.C.: The Associated Publishers, 1921), p. 252.

[4]Woodson, The History of the Negro Church, pp. 273, 298; S.P. Fullinwider, The Mind and Mood of Black America: 20th Century Thought (Homewood, Illinois: Dorsey Press, 1969), pp. 41-47; August Meier, Negro Thought in America 1880-1915 (Ann Arbor: Ann Arbor Paperbacks, 1973), pp. 182, 183-89, 220; Nancy J. Weiss, The National Urban League, 1910-1940 (New York: Oxford University Press, 1974), p. 26; Gayraud Wilmore, Black Religion and Black Radicalism, pp. 187-88; 191; Allan H. Spear, Black Chicago: The Making of a Ghetto, 1890-1920 (Chicago: The University of Chicago Press, 1967), p. 63; June Sochen, The Unbridgeable Gap: Blacks and Their Quest for the American Dream, 1900-1930 (Chicago: Rand McNally and Company, 1972), p. 15; Richard Bardolph, The Negro Vanguard (New York: Vantage Books, 1961), p. 145.

[5]Wills, "Aspects of Social Thought in the African Methodist Church, 1884-1910," hereafter "Aspects of Social Thought," pp. 235-62; "The Meaning of Racial Justice and the Limits of American Liberalism," The

Journal of Religious Ethics, pp. 199-215; and "Reverdy C. Ransom: The Making of an A.M.E. Bishop" in Randall K. Burkett and Richard Newman, eds., Black Apostles: Afro-American Clergy Confront the Twentieth Century (Boston: G.K. Hall & Co., 1978), pp. 181-205.

[6] Two doctoral dissertations on Ransom are currently in progress: Donald A. Drewett, "Ransom and Race: A Social, Political and Ecclesiastical Study, 1861-1959" (Drew University) and Frank E. Moorer, "Reverdy C. Ransom and the Transformation of the A.M.E. Church, 1860-1950" (John Hopkins University).

[7] Reverdy Cassius Ransom, Editorial: "The Thin Venner of Christianity on European Civilization," A.M.E. Review (October, 1914), pp. 195-99; Editorial: "Behold the Methodist," A.M.E. Review (January, 1917), p. 156; Editorial: "The Greatest Challenge to American Christianity?" A.M.E. Review (January 1917), pp. 157-59; The Negro: The Hope or Despair of Christianity (Boston: Ruth Hill Publishers, 1935), pp. 88-98; Preface to the History of the A.M.E. Church (Nashville: A.M.E. Sunday School Union, 1950), pp. 209-15.

[8] W. E. B. DuBois, ed. Atlanta University Studies, "The Negro Church" (Atlanta: Atlanta University Press, 1903), p. 123.

[9] Albert J. Raboteau, Slave Religion: The "Invisible Institution" in the Antebellum South (New York: Oxford University Press, 1978), p. ix. Raboteau's thesis appears to reflect the earlier view of E. Franklin Frazier's study, The Negro Church in America.

[10] W.E.B. DuBois, The Souls of Black Folk (New York: Fawcett Premier Books, 1961), pp. 142-44; Reverdy C. Ransom, "Editorial: The Influence of the Church on the Development and Progress of the American Negro," A.M.E. Review (April, 1918), pp. 259-60.

[11] Robert T. Handy, A Christian America (New York: Oxford University Press, 1971), p. 156.

[12] John A. Garraty, Interpreting American History: Part II, p. 56.

[13] Bardolph, Negro Vanguard, p. 140; Meier, Negro Thought, pp. 130-33; William G. Shade and Roy C. Herrenkohl, eds., Seven on Black: Reflections on the

Negro Experience in America (Philadelphia: J.B. Lippincott Co., 1969), pp. 96-98.

[14]W.E.B. DuBois, The Souls of Black Folk, p. 141.

[15]New York Amsterdam News, May 2, 1959., pp. 1, 9.

[16]Baltimore Afro-American, May 2, 1959, p. 1.

[17]Rayford W. Logan, ed., W.E.B. DuBois: A Profile (New York: Hill & Wang, 1971), pp. 320-21.

[18]William H. Ferris, The African Abroad of His Evolution in Western Civilization, Vol II (New Haven: The Tuttle Morehouse and Taylor Press, 1913), p. 794.

[19]John Daniels, In Freedom's Birthplace: A Study of the Boston Negro (Boston: Houghton Mifflin Co., 1914), p. 203; Alice M. Dunbar, Masterpieces of Negro Eloquence (New York: The Bookery Publishing Co, 1914), pp. 305-20; Carter G. Woodson, Negro Orators and Their Orations (Washington, D.C.: Associated Publishers, 1925), pp. 531-44; Marcus H. Bouleware, The Oratory of Negro Leaders: 1900-1968 (Westport, Connecticut; Negro Universities Press, 1969), pp. 51-52; Wilmore, Black Religion and Black Radicalism, p. 188.

[20]Ransom authored School Days at Wilberforce (Springfield, Ohio: The New Era Co., 1892); Disadvantages and Opportunities of Negro Youth (Cleveland: Thomas & Mattell, 1894); The Spirit of Freedom and Justice: Oration and Speeches (Nashville: A.M.E. Sunday School Union, 1926); The Negro: The Hope or the Despair of Christianity (Boston: Ruth Hill Publisher, 1935); Preface to the History of the A.M.E. Church (Nashville, A.M.E. Sunday School Union, 1950); and his autobiography, The Pilgrimage of Harriet Ransom's Son (Nashville: A.M.E. Sunday School Union, 195?). Ransom also periodically edited the Yearbook of Negro Churches during the 1930's and 1940's.

CHRONOLOGY OF REVERDY C. RANSOM

January 4, 1861	Born in Flushing, Ohio
1881	Married Leanna Watkins
1881	Entered Wilberforce University
1882	Transferred to Oberlin College
1883	Returned to Wilberforce University
1886	Graduated from Wilberforce University
1886	Divorced from Leanna Watkins
1886-88	Pastorate, Altoona and Hollisdaysburg, Pennsylvania
1887	Married Emma S. Conner
1888-90	Pastorate, Allegheny City, Pennsylvania
1890	Organized the first Men's Club and one of the first Epworth Leagues in the A.M.E. Church
1890-93	Pastorate, Springfield, Ohio
1893	Attended Columbian Exposition and World's Parliament of Religion, Chicago, Illinois
1893	Organized the first board of deaconnesses in the A.M.E. Church
1893-96	Pastorate, Cleveland, Ohio
1896-1900	Pastorate, Chicago, Illinois
1896	Attended the National Convention of United Society of Christian Endeavor in San Francisco California
1899	Participated in the National Convention of the Afro-American Council, Chicago, Illinois

10

1900	Founded the Institutional Church and Social Settlement in Chicago, Illinois
1900-04	Pastored Institutional Church and Social Settlement
1901	Attended the Ecumenical Conference of Methodism in London, England
1904	Pastorate, New Bedford, Massachusetts
1904-07	Pastorate, Boston, Massachusetts
1906	Delivered "John Brown" oration to the 2nd Annual meeting of the Niagara Movement at Harpers Ferry, Virginia
1907-12	Pastorate, New York, New York
1909	Participated in the Founding of the NAACP
1911	Attended the World Conference of Methodism in Toronto, Canada
1912-24	Editor of the A.M.E. Review
1913	Founded Church of Simon of Cyrene, New York, New York
1918	Unsuccessful bid for New York congressional seat
1921	Attended the World Conference of Methodism, London, England
1924	Elected Bishop of the A.M.E. Church
1932-52	Bishop of Third Episcopal District (Ohio, Western Pennsylvania and West Virginia) and Chairman, Wilberforce University Board of Trustees
1934	Founded with several other clergymen, the Fraternal Council of Negro Churches. Elected as its first president

11

1941	Death of second wife, Emma Ransom
1943	Married third wife, Georgia Myrtle Teal
1948-56	Historiographer of the A.M.E. Church
1952	Retired as active bishop
April 22, 1959	Died at his home, Tawawa Chimney Corner, Wilberforce, Ohio

CHAPTER I

From Log Cabin to University Classroom

MOTHER TO SON

Well, son, I'll tell you:
Life for me ain't been no
crystal stair.
It's had tacks in it,
And splinters,
And boards torn up,
And places with no carpet on
the floor--
Bare.
But all the time
I'se been a-climbin' on,
And reachin' landin's,
And turnin' corners,
And sometimes goin' in the
dark.
Where there ain't been no
light.
So boy, don't you turn your
back.
Don't you set down on the
steps.
'Cause you finds it's kinder
hard.
Don't you fall now--
For I'se still goin', honey,
I'se still climbin',
And life for me ain't been
no crystal stair.[1]

This volume is respectfully dedicated to the women of our race, and especially to the devoted, self-sacrificing mothers who moulded the lives of the subjects of these sketches, laboring and praying for their success.[2]

A greater meteor fell in Guernsey County, Ohio on May 1, 1860. It was studied and investigated by scientists all over the United States. Published accounts heralding its arrival appeared in newspapers and periodicals, East and West.[3] No such fanfare greeted the arrival of a black boy-child born "north of slavery," on January 4, 1861 in Flushing Village, Belmont County, Ohio.[4] When Reverdy Cassius Ransom entered the world, there was scant prospect that his life and existence would be any different from other black babies born in the America of that day because advancement of any kind was severely circumscribed for Blacks in 1861, North and South. The boundaries of their existence were hedged in by numerous legal and extra-legal restrictions. Thus segregated by custom and by law, Blacks were denied the vote, adequate education, equal justice, and employment opportunities.

Born in one of the states making up the Old Northwest Territory, Ransom was a member of a racial caste which John Hope Franklin has called the "American Anomaly," being "neither slave nor free." The status of the group from which Ransom came was at best tenuous. According to Franklin, white America's response to the ante-bellum Free Negro reflected its deep-seated prejudice toward Blacks generally, whether slave or "quasi-free."[5] Thus the response of white Ohioans to the presence of free Blacks who were settling in the state reflected the anti-Negro prejudice of the time. In spite of the fact that anti-slavery sentiment had developed within the Northwest Territory as early as the latter decades of the eighteenth century, the sentiment developed as opposition to the expansion of slavery. Few Ohioans argued for the eradication of the "peculiar institution." Lurking behind ostensible benign attitudes was the fear that the Old Northwest would be inundated by the immigration of manumitted slaves and free Blacks from the South. Several Northwest state legislatures enacted laws to stem the tide of immigration. For example, in 1804 and 1807, Ohio compelled Blacks entering the State to post a $1500.00 bond to guarantee their good behavior and to produce legal documents certifying their free status.[6] Reflecting the prevailing opinions in Ohio and in the Northwest region at the time of Ransom's birth, a Michigan editor wrote, "This government was made for the benefit of the white race...and not (for) Negroes."[7] Although Blacks had been in Ohio since the beginning of the century, they remained unwelcomed.[8]

The major migratory movement of Blacks into the Northwest Territory occurred between 1815 and 1850. Those decades were ones of heightened abolitionism, North and South, as the idealism of the Revolutionary War extended into the territories. Thus, while state legislatures passed laws easing the manumission of slaves, agricultural conditions also inadvertently aided the anti-slavery cause. Due to the exclusive cultivation of staple crops, the soil in the Upper South states of North Carolina and Virginia suffered severe erosion, thereby decreasing the economic impact of manumission in those states.[9]

The anti-slavery cause was also enhanced immeasurably by the reform crusade engendered by the revivalism of the Great Awakening. The Awakening aroused religious sentiment among many Christians favoring the abolition of slavery. Numerous Protestant denominations experienced schisms over the abolitionist issue.[10] Members of a sect with a long anti-slavery history, the Quakers of North Carolina and Virginia actively promoted the migration of southern Blacks to Ohio and the Northwest with the express purpose of establishing schools for them.[11]

Among those Blacks leaving Virginia and settling in Ohio was Reverdy C. Ransom's grandmother, Lucinda Johnson, who had been a slave in Virginia.[12] Although she had been freed some years earlier, Lucinda had been held in bondage illegally until given a sum of money and sent to Ohio. In 1847 she bought land on the outskirts of the little Quaker village of Flushing, Ohio and on it built "a house of hewn logs."[13] It was in this house that Ransom was born.[14] Ransom apparently had no knowledge of the identity of his father or of his paternal forebears and thanked George Warner Ransom, whom his mother married subsequent to his birth, for giving him a "surname." He said of his step-father, "This silent taciturn man was a father to me for more than fifty years."[15]

There is no doubt whatsoever concerning the identity of Reverdy's mother, though little factual data is extant about her. A native of Virginia, Harriet Ransom was 23 years old when she gave birth to Ransom. A domestic worker, she was a pivotal figure in her son's life. Ransom's determination to achieve emanated as much from the mind of Harriet as it did from his own.[16]

15

Ransom's most sharply etched memories of childhood included "constant hunger," the "cold" and the want associated with poverty. It was the "washing and toiling" of his mother that sustained and supported him. He remembered "no toys and little play," only work, any type of work that made survival possible.[17]

The community in which he lived was impoverished and consisted primarily of former slaves from the South, children of those ex-slaves and the descendants of the poorest rural Ohio Blacks of the Antebellum period. Practically all were employed in unskilled and menial occupations with almost no possibilities for improvement it their condition. Speaking of the community of his youth, Ransom recalled, "There was almost no high aspiration among the colored youth and nothing to inspire it."[18] When he expressed the ideals and aspirations of his mother, his friends would derisively call him a "white folks nigger."[19] It was against such a bleak and seemingly hopeless situation that Harriet Ransom and so many other black mothers of that generation struggled. Except for their perseverance and faith, the black generation following the Civil War would not have survived. This tenacity and courage prompted sociologist Jessie Bernard to dedicate Marriage and Family Among Negroes

> ...to Negro women, one of the most remarkable phenomena in American history. With a minimum of preparation, against all but impossible odds, these women have borne the major burden of pulling up the Negro population by its bootstraps. They have been spirited and independent, as well as self-sacrificing.[20]

These women faced immense obstacles in the rearing of their children. While there were few opportunities to encourage and motivate black youth in the Reconstruction period, there were numerous temptations available to them. Ransom, along with his peers, learned early to swear, and smoke, and steal. His mother, like many other religiously committed women, sought to counteract those influences by constantly urging her son to believe that a better future awaited him if he used his God-given capacities, especially his intelligence and personal integrity.

When Ransom was four years old, he and his mother

16

moved from his grandmother Lucinda's log cabin to his paternal step-grandfather Louis Ransom's log house in Washington Village, Guernsey County, Ohio. Harriet paid Ransom to board and care for her son while she worked. Reverdy was always hungry and quite unwelcome among the numerous Ransom children. His father's sister especially disliked him, rarely calling him by name, but referring to him as "you" or "that little red-haired devil."[21] Reverdy remembered the Ransom house as a place of many self-sufficient activities with his paternal step-grandmother, Betsy, making candles, lard and soft soap, carding and spinning wool as well as making her own dyes. All the women of the family except Harriet, smoked long-stemmed pipes and dipped snuff and "everbody drank whiskey." With the distillery near by, the children were often sent to get little tin buckets of whiskey which the family drank every morning before prayers and breakfast. All drank a toddy, including the children.[22] This may have been Ransom's introduction to the alcoholism that plagued him much of his life. Characteristically honest in assessing his problem, Ransom said, "This I found in after years to be a serious handicap to my reputation, my usefulness, and my spiritual power."[23]

Harriet and George moved to Cambridge, Ohio in 1869. This community revolved around the church. The Ransom family attended the African Methodist Episcopal Church regularly, where Harriet was an active member and participant. A.M.E. congregations had been organized in Ohio during the 1820's and 1830's. The vigorous evangelization drive was so successful that the state became an A.M.E. Episcopal headquarters in 1832. Growth in church membership accelerated after the Civil War when additional Blacks migrated to Ohio. Between 1865 and 1871, A.M.E. membership in the state increased 55 percent from 3,050 to 4,743.[24]

The church functioned as the primary social institution. It was there that the community met to share the occurences of daily life as well as worship. The importance of the church in the lives of those growing to adulthood during Reconstruction is attested to by Ransom's contemporaries, A.M.E. clerics Richard R. Wright, Jr. and Theophilus G. Steward. Wright described the community of his youth in Georgia as being pervaded by the church and Steward remembered his New Jersey community as consisting of three realities: the county school, the Sunday School, and the church.[25]

17

As the social and religious center of black life, the church was also the reflection of the best in racial leadership and development. While few models were available on the local level, national church leaders periodically visited the A.M.E. churches in Washington and Cambridge.[26] The Episcopal headquarters was located near Cambridge and was visited by contemporary A.M.E. leaders. Ransom remembered the visits of prominent A.M.E. clergy to the community of his youth.[27] These men epitomized the very highest in black leadership of that period. They were the molders of public opinion and their words carried great authority.

Thus, during Ransom's youth, the A.M.E. Church was an established institution in Ohio and the primary stabilizing influence in the Reconstruction black community. The A.M.E.s stressed black family life and uprightness and education. Inextricably tied to the commitment to the undergirding of the family was the church's commitment to education and learning. "The church and school generally stood side by side," Charles T. Hickok observed.[28] Frederick A. McGinnis, in The Education of the Negro in Ohio, suggested that the A.M.E. Church, in early nineteenth century Ohio, contributed the most to the education of black youth.[29] A.M.E. churches were often used as schoolhouses, and Ransom was educated in the A.M.E. Church of Cambridge. Harriet's church involvement may well have been motivated by the denomination's emphasis on education, which coincided with her long-term goal to educate her son.

Ransom grew up in a community with segregated schools. The schools supported by tax revenues seldom had school terms longer than five months, nor were proper school buildings provided. Classes for black students were usually held in church basements, sanctuaries, or in abandoned buildings where rent was at miniumum. Invariably, these schools offered inferior educational opportunities to their students.[30]

Ransom remebered his years in Cambridge's black public school, which met in the A.M.E. Church, as "noisy, undisciplined (and) ungraded." At thirteen, after her son had mastered what little had been taught in the school, Ransom's mother attempted to enroll him in the Cambridge Public School where Whites attended. The principal informed her that admission was impossible. Ransom later commented, "Since there was no where else to go, I remained in the colored school, covering the same ground year after year."[31] Mrs. Ransom was rebuffed once more when she tried to enroll her son in the Sunday School of the white Presbyterian Church in Cambridge.[32] Harriet Ransom was undaunted by her repeated failures, for she resolved that her son would acquire an education, and in this determination she never wavered, nor did she despair. With funds earned by taking in additional laundry work, Harriet paid several Whites to tutor her son in advanced subjects. Possessing an insatiable desire to learn algebra, Ransom succeeded in getting the owner of the town's shoe store to tutor him in return for his janitorial services.

His mother's experience as a domestic and washer-woman in the Cambridge homes of upper-class Whites strengthened her resolve that Reverdy would one day attend college, as did the young sons of her employers.[33] It was from the example of these upper-class Whites that she modelled the training of her son.

Ransom remembered his mother's attempts to encourage his emulation of the ideals, speech, and manners that she observed among her employers. In a few years, Harriet consented to her son's employment as a "houseboy" in the home of the cashier of the Cambridge bank. Ransom's experiences as a houseboy were far-reaching and significant in his further development, for he wrote, "The range of my reading became wider and more informing (and) I absorbed and assimilated the best I observed in these people and their friends who came and went."[34] Horace Mann Bond has observed that living in the household of Whites was in itself a "form of the process of acculturation" for black scholars when they were young.[35] Undoubtedly, Ransom's desire to continue his education was sustained by his employment, for he was the only black student taking advantage of a summer Normal School in 1879. Having taught in a short-term county school for two years, he stood ready to continue his quest for higher education. Therefore, his mother mortgaged her home in order to provide the necessary funds.[36]

Yet another obstacle temporarily obstructed Ransom's path to education-- "the ardor and passion of (a) young love." Her name was Leanna Watkins.[37] With Harriet's urging, they were married, both under legal

19

age, a few months before Ransom entered Wilberforce University.[38] A son, Harold George Ransom, was born some months after the marriage. The marriage was destined to fail, since Ransom's aspirations far out-distanced his wife's. In 1886, a divorce was secured by mutual consent, which gave Ransom "matrimonial release but not my freedom."[39] Ransom's abortive marital venture inflicted such life-long pain upon him that he rarely spoke about its effect. He described the experience as a "tragedy (housed in a) sealed room, the privacy of which no one is permitted to invade or disturb."[40] His mother took her grandson and raised him the first eight years of his life until her son's education had been completed and he was able to assume responsibility for the child.[41]

Ransom was able to overcome this personal crisis in his life with the assistance of his mother. Though individuals and events impacted his world and consciousness in later years, none of those influences were more pivotal than his early years with Harriet Ransom. He never forgot his childhood experiences of poverty, want, discrimination and prejudice, nor his mother's refusal to accept as perpetual, their economic or their racial circumstance. Therefore, his later sensitivity to the poor and his willingness to fight for racial and social justice were rooted in the courageous example of his mother. She was ever a source of encouragement, sustenance and comfort to him. Reminiscing near the end of his long life about his childhood memories of Christmas, Ransom wrote:

> The gift of Christ the Redeemer marks the beginning of a new day and a new world...Old as I am, it does not seem like Christmas if I do not get a stick of peppermint candy with a red stripe around it. Yes, the gates of memory open. I am a child again. Nostalgic emotions grip me while I chant:

> Backward turn backward oh time in your flight. Make me a child again just for tonight. Mother come back from that echoless shore. Take me in your arms again just as of yore. I am so weary of toil and of tears, Toil without recompense, tears all in vain, Over my slumbers your loving watch keep, Rock me to sleep, mother, rock me to sleep.[42]

20

Footnotes

[1] Langston Hughes, Selected Poems (New York: Alfred A. Knopf, 1965), p. 187.

[2] William J. Simmons, Men of Mark: Eminent, Progressive and Rising (1887); rpt. Chicago: Johnson Publishing Co., Inc., 1970), n.p.

[3] Charles Burleigh Galbreath, History of Ohio (New York: The American Historical Society, Inc., 1925), p. 354.

[4] Richard R. Wright, Jr., The Bishops of the African Methodist Episcopal Church (Nashville: A.M.E. Sunday School Union, 1963), p. 287, Reverdy C. Ransom, The Pilgrimage of Harriet Ransom's Son (Nashville: A.M.E. Sunday School Union, 195?), pp. 15-17.

[5] John Hope Franklin, From Slavery to Freedom (New York: Vintage Books, 1969), pp. 214-41. For information regarding Free Blacks in North and South, see Leon F. Litwak, North of Slavery (Chicago, The University of Chicago Press, 1961), and Ira Berlin, Slaves without Masters (New York: Vintage Books, 1976).

[6] Eugene H. Berwanger, The Frontier Against Slavery (Urbana: University of Illinois Press, 1967), pp. 1-2, 22, Charles T. Hickok, "The Negro in Ohio 1802-1870" (Ph.D. dissertation, Western Reserve University, 1896), pp. 32-76; Carter G. Woodson, A Century of Negro Migration (Washington, D.C.: Association for the Study of Negro Life and History, 1918), pp. 51-52; Leon F. Litwak, North of Slavery, pp. 72-74.

[7] Berwanger, The Frontier Against Slavery, p. 3. One of the ironies of "Jacksonian Democracy" involved the loss of political rights for free Blacks just as the ordinary white man was gaining the franchise. By 1860 most states, except for a few on the Atlantic seaboard, denied free Negroes the right to vote, to give evidence in court cases involving white men, to serve in state militias, to attend public schools with white children or to marry outside of their race.

[8] David A. Gerber, Black Ohio and the Color Line 1860-1915 (Urbana: University of Illinois Press, 1976), p. 4. In 1800, the black population of Ohio totalled 337, climbing to 9,568 or one percent of the

21

total population in 1830. In 1860, a year before Ransom's birth, Ohio's black population totalled 36,673 or 1.6 percent of the total population. Bureau of the Census, Negro Population 1790-1915 (New York: New York Times, 1968), pp. 44. See also Woodson, A Century of Negro Migration, pp. 3, 37-38.

[9]Winthrop Jordan, White Over Black: American Attitudes Toward the Negro 1550-1812 (Baltimore: Penguin Books, Inc., 1968), pp. 269-321; Woodson, A Century of Negro Migration, pp. 26-27; Gerber, Black Ohio, p. 19; Franklin, From Slavery to Freedom, pp. 126-44.

[10]Winthrop S. Hudson, Religion in America, 2nd ed. (New York: Charles Scribner's Sons, 1973), pp. 200-03.

[11]Carter G. Woodson, The Education of the Negro Prior to 1861 (New York: G.P. Putnam's Sons, 1915), p. 234; Woodson, A Century of Negro Migration, pp. 18-20; Jordan, White Over Black, pp. 271-76.

[12]The U.S. Bureau of the Census, Ohio 1860, Belmont County, Flushing Township lists 110 Blacks, 71 of whom were born in Virginia. It also lists a family headed by a Virginia-born Lucy Blanchard. Other sources give Lucinda's name as Johnson and Lewis. See "Bishop Ransom Honored with a Marble Plaque by His Native Town," August 12-13, 1950, n.p. Ransom Papers, Payne Seminary, The Cleveland Gazette, March 17, 1894, n.p.

[13]Lucinda's house and personal estate were valued at $240.00 and $50.00 respectively. U.S. Census for Ohio, 1860; Ransom, Pilgrimage, p. 15.

[14]Richard Bardolph, The Negro Vanguard (New York: Vintage Books, 1961), pp. 146-47; Ransom, Pilgrimage, p.15; Wright, The Bishops of the A.M.E. Church, p. 287.

[15]According to his Autobiography, Ransom suspected that he had Irish forebears. Bardolph states that his father was white. However, Ransom's third wife, Mrs. Georgia Teal Ransom, indicates that Ransom "knew his real father, who was a Negro (and) deeply resented" those who suggested otherwise. Ransom, Pilgrimage, pp. 16-17; Bardolph, Negro Vanguard, pp. 146-47; Interview with Mrs. Georgia Teal Ransom, Tawawa Chimney Corner, Wilberforce, Ohio, September 23, 1979.

[16]Interview with Mrs. Georgia Teal Ransom, Reverdy Ransom's third wife, Tawawa Chimney Corner, Wilberforce, Ohio, September 23, 1979.

[17]Ransom, "Confessions of a Bishop," Ebony 5 (March, 1950), p. 73; Gerber, Black Ohio, pp. 60-73.

[18]Ransom, Pilgrimage, p. 23.

[19]Ransom, Pilgrimage, p. 23; Gerber, Black Ohio, pp. 94-99.

[20]Jessie Bernard, Marriage and Family Among Negroes (Englewood Cliffs, New Jersey: Prentice Hall, Inc., 1966), p. x; E. Franklin Frazier, The Negro Family in the United States (1939 rpt. Chicago: University of Chicago Press, 1969), pp. 102-13.

[21]Ransom, Pilgrimage, p. 19.

[22]Ransom, "Confessions of a Bishop," Ebony, p. 73; Pilgrimage, pp. 19-20.

[23]Ransom, Pilgrimage, p. 48.

[24]Daniel A. Payne, History of the A.M.E. Church, ed. C.S. Smith (Nashville, 1891) pp. 44, 97, 118, 180, 205; Gerber, Black Ohio, pp. 20, 141, 142.

[25]Richard R. Wright, Jr., 87 Years Behind the Black Curtain: An Autobiography (Nashville: A.M.E. Sunday School Union, 1963) pp. 76-78; Theophilus G. Steward, Fifty Years in the Gospel Ministry (Philadelphia: A.M.E. Book Concern, 1914), p. xi. For other indications of the church's prominence in Ante-bellum and Reconstruction black life, see Franklin, From Slavery to Freedom, p. 27; Litwak, North of Slavery, pp. 187-89.

[26]Wayne S. Snider, Guernsey County's Black Pioneers, Patriots, and Persons (Columbus: Ohio Historical Society, 1979), pp. 87-89.

[27]Ransom, Pilgrimage, p. 23.

[28]Hickok, "The Negro in Ohio, 1803-1870," p. 85.

[29]Frederick A. McGinnis, The Education of the Negro in Ohio (Blanchester, Ohio: Curless Publishing

Co., 1962), p. 27.

[30]Hickok, "The Negro in Ohio, 1802-1870," pp. 79, 104. Because of working conditions and poor financing of their schools, Blacks attended school irregularly. Gerber, Black Ohio, p. 97.

[31]Ransom, Pilgrimage, p. 22; W oodson, Education of the Negro, pp. 237, 240: Hickok, "The Negro in Ohio, 1802-1870," p. 107. Records of the Cambridge School Board for 1858 indicated a school for Blacks. Ten years later, the Cambridge School Board was renting the "African Church" for its "colored" pupils. Snider, Guernsey County's Black Pioneers, pp. 78, 78-79, 82.

[32]Ransom, Pilgrimage, p. 24.

[33]Ransom, Pilgrimage, pp. 21-22.

[34]Ransom, Pilgrimage, pp. 25-26.

[35]Horace Mann Bond, Black American Scholars: A Study of Their Beginnings (Detroit: Balcamp Publishing, 1972), p. 38. Harriet was reported to have augmented Reverdys' acculturation process with a "relentless course in How to Carry and Conduct Yourself." Cleveland Call and Post, June 25, 1956, n.p. Ransom, Papers, (Payne Seminary Archives).

[36]Ransom, Pilgrimage, p. 26; Ransom papers at Tawawa Chimney Corner, Wilberforce, Ohio.

[37]Ransom, Pilgrimage, p. 26.

[38]Ransom, "Confessions of a Bishop," Ebony, p. 73.

[39]Ransom, Pilgrimage, pp. 26-27; "Confessions of a Bishop," Ebony, p. 73.

[40]Ransom, Pilgrimage, p. 26.

[41]Ransom, Pilgrimage, p. 27; "Confessions of a Bishop," Ebony, p. 73.

[42]Ransom, "A Christmas Meditation," undated, pp. 1-2. Ransom Papers, Wilberforce University Archives.

CHAPTER II

To Respect Black

I entered Wilberforce in the Fall
of 1881, to be enveloped by this
atmosphere and environment....In
those days, Wilberforce was a
praying school, which read its
Bible, sang lustily and went to
church and Sunday School each
Sunday. Not learning, but
Religion came first. After that
came service to one's race and
country. Most all seemed very
much in earnest about those
things. Racial equality was
taught, believed in, and
practiced as far as possible.
Racial self-confidence, self-
respect, dignity, honor, the
ambition to achieve in every
line of endeavor, were taught
and encouraged.[1]

In September 1881, Ransom matriculated at Wilberforce University. However, he was evidently not satisfied with what he found at Wilberforce since he decided that he could find "better opportunity for self-help, together with broader and more liberal educational advantages at Oberlin College."[2] Ransom entered Oberlin College in the fall of 1882, receiving a small tuition scholarship.[3] Other factors may have also encouraged his attendance at Oberlin. For example, W.S. Scarborough, perhaps the most accomplished scholar on the faculty at Wilberforce, had graduated from Oberlin in 1875. The year following his graduation, Scarborough accepted an appointment to teach at Wilberforce, where he spent his entire career.[4] In addition to Professor Scarborough, there were other persons at Wilberforce who may have influenced Ransom to matriculate at Oberlin. John M. Langston, a long-time resident of Wilberforce and an 1849 graduate of Oberlin, may have also influenced Ransom's decision. Lawyer, law school dean, college president, diplomat and congressman, Langston was considered second only to Frederick Douglass in prominence and prestige.[5] It is, however, much more probable that Ransom's decision to leave Wilberforce was largely his own. During his youth, except for his mother, the persons most responsible for awakening his intellect were white. White Oberlin may have may have loomed in his mind as better equipped to provide him a top-flight education than black Wilberforce. Before arriving at Wilberforce, Ransom observed that he had never seen a "colored professor" and admitted that he had had "little faith in the capacity of men and women of his race (when it came to) the exercise of the higher and nobler power of man."[6]

Ransom's struggle for an education continued at Oberlin, where, to support himself he held several jobs simultaneously: he worked for a private family, earning his board and lodging; sawed wood for twenty-five cents an hour; and worked as a porter in a barbershop.[7] While at Oberlin, Ransom attended lectures given by national figures. He also remembered several of his black classmates, such as Mary Church (Terrell) and Ralph Langston, son of John M. Langston, who would distinguish themselves in the struggle for justice.

Though Ransom did find higher educational standards and a higher general atmosphere of culture at Oberlin, he also discovered subtle forms of discrimination there which prevented black students from participating in

26

campus activities.[8] The historic liberalism and tolerance of Oberlin seemed not to have been much in evidence during Ransom's stay.[9] He addressed a meeting he helped to organize at Oberlin "to protest a new regulation segregating colored girls at a separate table in the ladies' dining hall." Soon thereafter, Ransom's scholarship was withdrawn by the faculty.[10] The following year he was back at Wilberforce. Ransom's return to Wilberforce compelled him to acknowledge with deeper appreciation and confidence the heritage and promise of the institution.

The university was located in Green County, Ohio. The community in which Wilberforce was established had been settled during the 1840's and 1850's by fugitive slaves, free Blacks, and the racially mixed families of southern slaveowners.[11] Among its distinct geographical features, located among a beautiful countryside, were numerous streams and springs. Wealthy Blacks as well as southern masters, with their "wives, consorts," and their mulatto children, were attracted to the area.[12] The establishment of Wilberforce University in 1856 by the Methodist Episcopal Church made the community especially attractive to planters who wished to educate their mulatto children, and thus, before the outbreak of the Civil War, the institution primarily served the educational needs of that constituency,[13] and functioned much like a preparatory school. However, the Civil War severely strained the resources of the university and made the attendance of students from the South and the means to support their education impossible. The school was forced to close in 1862.[14] In spite of the financial difficulties, Bishop Daniel Alexander Payne, who had served on Wilberforce's Board of Trustees as well as its Executive Committee, saw the opportunity to purchase the university for the sum of $10,000 in order to provide training in higher education for the clergy and laity of the A.M.E. Church.[15]

Consequently, the names of Payne and Wilberforce became synonymous and the "scholar" bishop committed the remainder of his life to the advocacy of an educated ministry.[16] Payne, a man of intense piety and a strong believer in moral purity and perfection, served as the first black president of Wilberforce. He believed that religion constituted the only true foundation for living. Therefore, Payne envisioned the purpose of Wilberforce to be the training of men and women for

27

Christian living through service. When Ransom attended
Wilberforce just two decades after its founding, the
university's purpose remained unaltered.

Wilberforce University was also a residential
community for members of its faculty and their families.
Many faculty would later become A.M.E. bishops.
Included were men such as James A. Shorter, Benjamin F.
Lee, and Benjamin W. Arnett who were important
influences in Ransom's life. The community embodied the
finest in black Christian culture and attracted the
attention of many black spokesmen of the day, some of
whom not only applauded its solidarity and life-style,
but moved their families there.

Of the many families attracted to the Wilberforce
community, none was more esteemed than that of Martin
Delaney. Founder and co-editor with Frederick Douglass
of The North Star, Delaney was a nationally known
lecturer, physician, scientist, soldier, and
emigrationist. His book, The Condition, Elevation,
Emigration and Destiny of the Colored People of the
United States, Politically Considered, is a definitive
explication of black nationalism. Delaney was impressed
by the Wilberforce community, the core of which was a
black university founded and sustained by a black
religious denomination, and he chose to settle there in
1864. Wilberforce was an ideal community fo r one who
maintained the importance of "black nationality, black
pride, and black Africa."[17] Wilberforce was not only a
place steeped in the commitment of learning and
knowledge, which Delaney affirmed, but it was also a
place where Blacks governed themselves while existing on
amenable terms with their white neighbors. Thus, it
appeared that Wilberforce was creating an ideal
community in which black family life could be nurtured
and developed. One of the university's first graduates,
Hallie Q. Brown, agreed that the community "attracted
the best element of colored people."[18]

Ransom's experience within the Wilberforce
community greatly influenced his ideas on the importance
of black family life, black institutions, and the
personhood of Blacks. The depth of the community's
effect on Ransom is displayed when he writes, "This
college and community are a verification of the Negro's
humanity and manhood. It proves that darkest centuries
of heathenism, and other centuries black with crimes
against the life of the soul, have not been able to rob

28

the Negro of his humanity or destroy within him the image of God."[19] Daniel Payne, the community's most revered inhabitant, most certainly concurred.

Payne not only founded Wilberforce, but also established its educational philosophy. He believed that true education developed moral character and Christian piety. During Ransom's years, Wilberforce continued to primarily stress religious training and then academic training. Bible study was emphasized and students were required to attend chapel twice a day. There were two prayer meetings held each week, one of which was compulsory. Temperance was advocated so strongly that students were required to recite Scriptural verses relating to the subject.[20]

Student social life at Wilberforce was also severely restricted. According to the 1884 Wilberforce Catalogue, "All practices tending to immorality were forbidden (since) the school's aim was to inspire and increase in the pupil self-respect and self-development"[21] Association with the opposite sex was forbidden to the extent that two reading rooms, one for each sex, were instituted. The use of intoxicating beverages, tobacco, games of chance, profanity and obscenity were strictly forbidden. Furthermore, visiting off-campus families, fellow student's rooms or the kitchen without permission was also prohibited.[22] Although Ransom seems to have chafed somewhat under the restrictive atmosphere, his recollections of Wilberforce were generally positive.

When Ransom attended the university, the student population was relatively small, averaging in attendance 147 during the years 1876-1884 and 220 during the years 1884 to 1899. Unfortunately, the attrition was high. A few years later, Ransom criticized those students who failed to complete the full theological course of study. He believed that they were shirking their responsibilities to the church and the race. In Ransom's view, education was absolutely essential to the advancement of the race, and black ministers, above all, required excellent preparation. He challenged the students to fully prepare themselves to minister in an increasingly complex society, where traditional religious practices would no longer suffice.[23]

The theological department into which Ransom enrolled was a four year course of study comparable to most theological curricula of the day. The curriculum

29

combined collegiate and theological courses among which were natural history, philosophy of history, chemistry, geology, systematic theology, Ethics, Greek and Hebrew.[24]

During the 1884-85 academic term, eight students were enrolled in the theological department at levels levels from the first to the third year of studies.[25] Employing both the inductive and deductive methods, the theological course allowed the widest liberty of investigation and of expression, "excepting that which borders upon impiety and blasphemy."[26] The aim of the curriculum was to train ministers "broadly and scientifically (so) that they would have greater ability to meet and vanquish modern infidelity."[27] Soon after graduation from Wilberforce, Ransom challenged his ministerial peers to prepare themselves to speak intelligently to issues of the times.[28]

Looking back at his years at Wilberforce, Ransom remembered with most pleasure his participation in the Sodalian Society, a campus organization devoted to literary discussion, debate, rhetoric, and the development of oratorical skills. Members of the Sodalian Society were exposed to "merciless" criticism by peers and faculty. If a person possessed deficiencies of any kind, they were quickly revealed. Ransom undoubtedly savored the challenge to excellence which membership in the society required. While much effort was given to literary composition, it was in oratory that most students sought to excel. The society, organized in 1871, adopted as its motto, "We study not for school, but for life."[29] In 1885, Ransom was vice-president of the Sodalian Society, which was the school's most prestigious student organization. The oratorical brilliance which would bring Ransom fame was nourished by his participation in the Society.

Ransom's later success depended, in part, upon yet another Wilberforce influence, the Reverend Benjamin W. Arnett. Arnett's interests were wide-ranging. His spiritual and political affairs represented only his most visible involvement. He served on the Executive Committee of the National Sociological Society, was trustee of the United Society of Christian Endeavor, and was delegate to the International Convention of the YMCA in 1871. As a bibliophile, Arnett acquired one of the largest collections then in existence of rare and contemporary books by and about black people. He had an interest in history, which manifested itself not only in his library holdings, but also in the histories he wrote of the various churches he pastored. He was a trustee of the Archeological and Historical Society of Ohio. Arnett was considered a great preacher and orator and was elected historiographer and bishop of the A.M.E. Church.

Born in Pennsylvania, Arnett was elevated to the episcopacy of the A.M.E. Church in 1888, two years after Ransom's graduation from Wilberforce. According to one A.M.E. cleric and historian, George A. Singleton, Arnett's contributions to his denomination were illustrious and enduring.[31] Arnett, one of the most popular and influential ministers of his day, served black people both ecclesiastically and politically. At the World Parliament of Religion held in Chicago in 1893, a part of the World's Columbian Exposition, Arnett was so influential and well-known that he was the only Black chosen to address that religious convocation.[32] In 1901, Arnett presided at the Ecumenical Conference of Methodism in London, a gathering which Ransom attended through Arnett's influence.[33] As a politician, Arnett was no less well-known; he was actively involved in the Republican Party and was a leader in the black convention movement in Pennsylvania during Reconstruction. A delegate to its National Convention in 1864, Arnett's political acumen was further recognized when the National Convention of Colored Men, meeting in Washington, D.C. in 1867, chose him as secretary. Arnett was elected to the Ohio State Legislature in 1885 and played a key role in the passage of Ohio's Civil Rights Act of 1886. The Civil Rights Act repealed the state's harsh Black Law Codes. Such Codes had, among other things, legalized segregated schooling and transportation.[34]

As Chaplain of the 1896 Republican National Convention in St. Louis, Arnett was considered a close confidante and adviser of Ohio's G.O.P. boss, Mark Hanna, and consequently, of Hanna's protege, William McKinley.[35] Richard R. Wright considered Arnett to be one of the most powerful black political advisers to President William McKinley.[36] Ransom could not have found a more influential friend and supporter than Benjamin W. Arnett. Ransom probably worked for Arnett while attending Wilberforce and may have assisted Arnett in his historical research and speech writing. In the years that followed, Arnett appointed Ransom to Bethel

A.M.E. Church in Chicago and helped make possible the denominational funds with which Ransom founded the Institutional Church and Social Settlement. Arnett was a trusted and reliable friend to Ransom up until his death in 1906. Both men treasured the friendship they shared.[37]

Thus Wilberforce University and the surrounding community provided the atmosphere for Ransom's intellectual, social and spiritual development. During his first year at Wilberforce, Ransom had a significant religious experience. He received the "call" to the ministry. Although Harriet Ransom had raised her son in the best Christian milieu she could obtain, the emotionalism often associated with conversion offended Ransom's sensibilities. He remembered that he could never "decide (whether) to go to the mourner's bench and kneel on the bare floor with a great crowd of singing, shouting, perspiring men and women surrounding me."[38] It was during the quiet of a Wilberforce night that Ransom realized the direction for his life. Later, in speaking about his call to the ministry, Ransom described this experience as "one of those rapturous moments, not told by tongue or pen, when earth and heaven meet and blend in happy consciousness that God has entered into our life, making himself (sic) known."[39] That Ransom was in conflict with traditional methods of personal evangelism is attested to by his refusal to submit to the blandishments of "a great crowd of singing, shouting, perspiring men and women." However, he was not alone in his aversion, for many other incipient Social Gospelers experienced a certain disquiet regarding the religious orthodoxy of the day.[40] Ransom was certainly troubled by orthodox formuations regarding science.

He remembered his theology professor, Thomas H. Jackson, as being so orthodox that "the science of evolution was anathema" to him. Jackson also denied the science of geology and tenaciously held to the literal account of the creation found in Genesis.[41] Ransom was amenable to the new sciences and dismayed by Jackson's obstinate refusal to even consider them. However, he remained silent about the misgivings since "there were no sympathetic human counsellors to whom I could go."[42] Thus, instead of sharing his doubts about the efficacy of his call with particular reference to his inability to affirm all of church dogma, Ransom read the Bible, a wide assortment of books, and with "the knowledge that these doctrines were man-made,

32

(acquired) both confidence and courage to obey and follow the inner voice."[43]

One can sense in the following poem written during this crisis, Ransom's determined struggle to respond with integrity to the call:

I will not, though it raise me to the skies
With deceitful heart on holy things arise,
I will not into God's pure temple sneak,
And there proclaim His tiding once a week,
When not within my soul the Spirit's voice
Has named me as His messenger of choice.
Though I have thought, when once into the race,
I'd fill God's alter with eloquence and grace,
Though raptured thousands came to sing my praise
While I on high my wavering voice shall raise.
I'd rather let men's praise go unsung
Than post a seraph with a devil's tongue;
I'd rather dwell in poverty obscure
And all the pangs of poverty endure,
Than for all the honors which Church can give,
Through life a timorous hypocrite to live.
How many hearts through life with burdens go,
The gospel seeds in other hearts to sow
Afraid to face the world with honest look
And own that they their calling have mistook.
I'd rather let the world look on in scorn,
While I may fall below ambition's dream
Nor reach the goal which my high hopes have seen;
I'll have not through life been toying with His
Word.[44]

Thus, Ransom's life and ministry must be viewed from the perspective of his own religious awareness and understanding. His later openness to Social Gospel theories was but an extenstion of earlier struggles to integrate the "new science" into a meaningful faith and ministry. It is also clear that Ransom was not impressed by outward forms of religiosity; by shouting, pious platitudes or theological statements, but by the actions of persons professing an inward summons. Therefore, his commitments over the years, whether in the local church, denominational and ecumenical associations, various protest organizations and political parties, were outward manifestations of an inward call. His actions always emanated from religious convictions. Ransom acknowledged the university's significant role in this religious awareness when he stated, "...A knowledge of the conscious, inward presence of God was worth more to me than all other things gained... at Wilberforce...Any system of education that leaves this untouched and unaroused, ignores the fountain of strength and power upon which knowledge should lean for its right application to the businesss of life."[45]

In March, 1886, it was decided by faculty vote to allow Ransom, among others, to graduate, provided he completed work in Systematic Theology and Astronomy. When the faculty averaged the grades of the ten prospective graduates, Ransom's rank of 87 was the third higest in the class.[46] The class of '86 was considered by a reporter for the Christian Recorder to have been the finest in the university's short history. The highlight of the Commencement week's activities was the Sodalian Literary Society's oration delivered on "individuality" by Ransom. The Christian Recorder correspondent considered the speech the best ever delivered by a student and revealed that "the audience was fairly swayed by the speaker whose polised language moved the assembly dozens of times to burst forth in deafening applause."[47]

On Thursday, June 17, 1886, Ransom graduated from Wilberforce, delivering an oration entitled "Civil and Divine Law." Upon graduation, Ransom remarked that he and his mother "had graduated together."[48] Thus, when Ransom left Wilberforce, he was imbued with ideals of moral, educational and social uplift for black people. The university's "aim (was) to make Christian scholars, not mere bookworms, but workers, educated workers with Goᴅ for man."[49] With the convictions gained from Wilberforce, he set out to test the theological and social ideas learned there in the world of action.

34

[1] Reverdy C. Ransom, The Pilgrimage of Harriet Ransom's Son, pp. 23.

[2] Bardolph, The Negro Vanguard, pp. 154-55; Wright, Bishops of the A.M.E. Church, pp. 287-88; Ransom, Pilgrimage, p. 33.

[3] Receiving "incidentals" from an Avery scholarship, Ransom was enrolled in Oberlin's Preparatory Middle Class. W.E. Bigglestone, archivist, Oberlin College to Calvin S. Morris, January 29, 1980. According to the Oberlin College Catalogue for 1882-83, his courses included Latin Prose Composition, Greek Grammar, Science of Governmen, Cicero, Two Orations and History of Greece and Rome.

[4] For a discussion of Scarborough's years at Oberlin and Wilberforce, see Francis P. Weisenberger, "William Sanders Scarborough: Early Life and Years at Wilberforce," Ohio History, Vol. 71, No. 3, October, 1962, pp. 211-14; Bardolph, Negro Vanguard, p. 291; Simmons, Men of Mark, pp. 417-18. Frederick A. McGinnis, A History and an Interpretation of Wilberforce University (Blanchester, Ohio: Brown Publishing Co, 1941), pp. 145-46.

[5] William J. Simmons, Men of Mark, pp. 345-52; August Meier, Negro Thought in America: 1880-1915 (Ann Arbor, Michigan: Ann Arbor Paperbacks, 1966), p. 78; Herbert Aptheker, ed., A Documentary History of the Negro People in the United States (New York: The Citadel Press, 1969), p. 423; McGinnis Education of the Negro in Ohio, p. 80.

[6] Ransom, School Days at Wilberforce (Springfield, Ohio: New Era, 1890), p. 19.

[7] Ransom, Pilgrimage, p. 33; Bardolph, Negro Vanguard, p. 155.

[8] Ransom, Pilgrimage, p. 40.

[9] W. E. Bigglestone, "Oberin College and the Negro Student, 1865-1940" Journal of Negro History, Vol. 86, No. 3, July, 1971, pp. 198-200.

[10] The "segregated seating" incident occured during

the school year of 1882-1883 as Ransom remembered. Complaints by white students about eating with black students became so frequent by the fall of 1882 that Blacks were seated at a table by themselves. After much debate and disturbance, the school's president abolished the separate seating arrangements. By that time Ransom was gone. Oberlin has no record of his dismissal or his involvement in the protest. Bigglestone, "Oberlin College and the Negro Student," p. 200; Ransom, Pilgrimage, p. 33; Bardolph, Negro Vanguard, p. 155; Wright, Bishops of the A.M.E. Church, p. 288.

[11]The A.M.E. Church established Union Seminary, Columbus, Ohio in the 1840's. When the denomination purchased Wilberforce in 1863, the Seminary was merged with it. Carter G. Woodson, The History of the Negro Church, 1921, rpt. (Washington, D.C.: The Associated Publishers, 1972), pp. 148, 181, 184. McGinnis, The Education of Negroes in Ohio, pp. 83-84.

[12]John Hope Franklin, From Slavery to Freedom: A History of Negro Americans, 3rd edition (New York: Vintage Books, 1969), p. 226; Edward Reuter, The Mulatto in the United States, 1918 rpt. (New York: Negro Universities Press, 1969).

[13]Horace Talbert, Sons of Allen: Together with a Sketch of the Rise and Progess of Wilberforce University (Xenia, Ohio: Aldine Press, 1906), pp. 266-68. E. Franklin Frazier, The Negro in the United States (New York: MacMillan Co., 1949), p. 451; Gerber, Black Ohio and the Color Line, pp. 19, 127; McGinnis, The Education of Negroes in Ohio, pp. 36-37; Franklin, From Slavery to Freedom, p. 231.

[14]Daniel A. Payne, Recollections of Seventy Years (1888; rpt. New York: Arno Press and the New York Times, 1969), p. 152; Hallie Q. Brown, Pen Pictures of Pioneers of Wilberforce (Xenia, Ohio: Aldine Press, 1937), p. 82; Woodson, Education of the Negro Prior to 1861, pp. 272-74; Woodson, History of the Negro Church, p. 181; Talbert, Sons of Allen, pp. 268-69.

[15]Arthur Paul Stokes, "Daniel Alexander Payne: Churchman and Educator" Ph.D. dissertation, Ohio State University, 1973), p. 144; McGinnis, Education of the Negro in Ohio, pp. 83-84; Payne, Recollections, pp. 150-54; Woodson, History of the Negro Church, p. 181.

[16]William J. Simmons, _Men of Mark_, pp. 779-83; Bardolph, _The Negro Vanguard_, p. 106; Brown, _Pen Pictures_, p. 68.

[17]Victor Ullman, _Martin R. Delaney: The Beginning of Black Nationalism_ (Boston: Beacon Press, 1971), pp. 291-92; Ransom, _Pilgrimage_, p. 31. Daniel Payne said of Delaney, "If his love for humanity had been as strong as his love of race, his influence would have been greater." Payne, _Recollections of Seventy Years_, p. 160.

[18]Brown, _Pen Pictures_, p. 89. Brown graduated in Wilberforce's first class in 1870. Talbert, _Sons of Allen_, p. 274.

[19]Ransom, _School Days_, p. 36.

[20]Ransom, _Pilgrimage_, p. 31; McGinnis, _A History and an Interpretation_, p. 45; Brown, _Pen Pictures_, pp. 10-12.

[21]Benjamin F. Lee, _Sketch of Wilberforce_ (Xenia, Ohio: Torchlight Job Rooms, 1884), Wilberforce University, pp. 9-10, 13-14.

[22]Much faculty time and effort was expended disciplining and discussing the minor and major infractions of Wilberforce students. See Faculty Minutes, 1885-1890, Wilberforce Unversity Archives, Wilberforce, Ohio; Mary Church Terrell, _A Colored Woman in a White World_ (Washington, D.C.: National Association of Colored Women's Clubs, Inc., 1968), p. 61; McGinnis, _History and Intepretation_, p. 161.

[23]_Ninth Quadrennial Report of Wilberforce University_, 1900, p. 7. Ransom criticized those students who failed to complete their full course of study. Ransom, "Why This Haste?" _Christian Recorder_, 37 (August 28, 1890), p. 1.

[24]Biennial Catalogue, 1883, pp. 18-19, Wilberforce University Archives, Wilberforce, Ohio; McGinnis, _History and Interpretation_.

[25]_Wilberforce University Catalogue_, 1884-85, pp. 13, 10, Wilberforce University Archives.

[26]Benjamin W. Arnett, S.T. Mitchell, _The Wilberforce Alumnal_ (Xenia, Ohio: The Gazette Printing

Co., 1885), pp. 22-23.

[27]*Biennial Catalogue*, Wilberforce University, 1883, Wilberforce University Archives, pp. 18-19.

[28]Ransom, "Too Cultured for His Flock," *Christian Recorder*, 34 (November 18, 1887), pp. 1-2.

[29]Ransom, *School Days*, pp. 54-55; McGinnis, *History and Interpretation*, p. 49.

[30]Meier, *Negro Thought in America*, p. 57; Bardolph, *Negro Vanguard*, p. 101; Woodson, *History of the Negro Church*, p. 212; Wright, *Bishops of the A.M.E. Church*, pp. 78-79.

[31]George A. Singleton, *The Romance of African Methodism: A Study of the African Methodist Episcopal Church* (New York: Exposition Press, 1952), p. 129.

[32]Wright, *Bishops of the A.M.E. Church*, p. 78; Ransom, *Pilgrimage*, pp. 59-60.

[33]Ransom, *Pilgrimage*, pp. 93-95.

[34]Simmons, *Men of Mark*, pp. 625-31; Meier, *Negro Thought*, pp. 51, 71.

[35]Wright, *Bishops*, p. 82.

[36]Arnett was not without competitors in the struggle for black political leadership. George A. Myers, a wealthy barber and Harry Smith, ascerbic newspaper editor and Ohio Republican legislator, were his two most prominent rivals for leadership. Gerber, *Black Ohio*, pp. 345-70; Felix James, "The Civic and Political Activities of George A. Myers," *Journal of Negro History*, 58 (April, 1973), pp. 166-78.

[37]Singleton, *Romance*, p. 129; Interview with Georgia Teal Ransom, September 23, 1979.

[38]Ransom, *Pilgrimage*, p. 32. Two of Ransom's Social Gospel compatriots experienced similar aversions to the old-time religious conversion. See R.R. Wright, *87 Years Behind the Black Curtain* (Nashville: A.M.E. Sunday School Union, 1865), p. 79; and On Washington Gladden's struggle "to come through;" see Henry F. May, *Protestant Churches and Industrial America* (New York:

Harper & Brothers, 1949), p. 171.

[39]Ransom, _Pilgrimage_, pp. 31-32.

[40]Ransom, _Pilgrimage_, p. 38; Henry F. May,
Protestant Churches and Industrial America, p. 171.

[41]Ransom, _Pilgrimage_, p. 38.

[42]Ransom, _Pilgrimage_, p. 38.

[43]Ransom, _Pilgrimage_, p. 38.

[44]Ransom, _Pilgrimage_, pp. 38-39.

[45]Ransom, _Pilgrimage_, pp. 32-33.

[46]_Faculty Minutes, Wilberforce University_, March
24, May 11, 1886. Wilberforce University Archives.

[47]John G. Brown, "Wilberforce University:
Twenty-Third Commencement Exercises - A Brilliant
Closing," _Christian Recorder_, 24 (July 8, 1886), p. 1.

[48]Ransom, _Pilgrimage_, p. 42.

[49]Arnett and Mitchell, _The Wilberforce Alumnal_,
pp. 22-23.

CHAPTER III

Intellectual Pilgrimage and Outlook

It is not simply "an act of justice...it
is an act of almighty God--that all men
are, and should be free. To intefere
with this is to usurp the sovereignty
which God has conferred upon men on this
earth."[1]

We must view Reverdy Ransom's life and thought as a product of a specific social and intellectual history. We are not simply looking at what he experienced, but how he and others perceived the experience. In so doing, we must also look at how Ransom's contemporaries understood their world, and, again, at the consciousness that was possible for his time--after Darwin, before Freud, and during the period when Marx's Capital and socialism were rigorously debated by the educated. Ransom's thought and action must be read against the constraints of a "for Whites only" American society and simultaneously within the context of the intellectual history of the time. This involves an awareness of the two main currents to which he was exposed during the 1880's and 1890's: the Social Gospel and the deteriorating position of black people in the United States and Africa.

Concern and interest in the rights of labor were perhaps the Social Gospel's major preoccupation over the years as it urged better working conditions and higher wages primarily for European immigrants. While Ransom shared the Social Gospel Movement's commitment to the working class, the primary focus of his concern was the employment dilemma faced by Blacks who were denied employment opportunites by the racist practices of both industry and labor.

With this deep concern about the effects of multinational capitalism on workers, many Social Gospelers were attracted to socialism as the most effective solution to world problems. What they embraced, however, was a Christianized version of socialism. Jesus, not Marx, remained their example, as he called man into a proper relationship with God, which meant specifically to love both God and one's neighbor. One Social Gospeler, the Reverend Frank N. North, declared that "the common brotherhood of man is at once the Gospel of Christianity and the Gospel of Socialism."[2] Socialism was the spirit of the age and through it the church was to prove its faith and apply its principles to life. Thus, socialism became a social means to a spiritual end for those Christians, the fundamental purpose of which was to awaken the church to its social duty.[3]

Even more uncompromising in their advocacy of societal transformation were the followers of the radical Christian socialist and dynamic preacher and

and professor, George D. Herron. Probably the most well-known radical Social Gospeler of the 1890's, Herron lectured and preached to countless college audiences and church congregations during that decade. A founder of the American Institute of Sociology, Herron was also a founder of the American Institute of Sociology, Herron was also a founding editor of the Social Gospel journal, the Kingdom.

According to Herron, men of wealth could begin to solve pressing social problems by becoming disciples of Christ. Using the early church as his model for Christian socialism, Herron wrote that "the public ownership of the sources and means of production is the sole answer to the social question and the sole basis of spiritual liberty."[4] As his views became decidedly socialistic rather than Christian in emphasis, his effectiveness within church circles diminished by the beginning of the century. Nevertheless, Herron influenced countless individuals during the preceding decade. Not least among them was Reverdy C. Ransom.

Ransom had quite possibly heard Herron lecture to the Christian Leadership Citzenship League of Chicago during the last three months of 1898. If not, Ransom was fully aware of Herron's many articles and books, particularly Between Caesar and Jesus, (1899).[5] The book was a compilation of the eight Monday afternoon lectures Herron had given in Chicago for the Christian Leadership Citizenship League in 1898.

Besides Herron, the ideas extant in the late 19th century America exposed Ransom to the ideas and precepts of social Christianity. Henry George's influential and captivating work, Progress and Poverty (1879) critically analyzed the misery and suffering of those who toiled for their livelihood in the midst of enormous wealth. His book, a synthesis of economics, ethics and religion, denied employers the right to pay their employees a substandard wage and argued against the religious viewpoint that God had sacrificed weaker individuals to stronger men in order to perfect a superior race. No admirer of socialism and often in conflict with it, George appealed to the church from the vantage point of a deeply committed Christian. His influence extended to Social Gosepl leaders, including Josiah Strong, William Dwight Porter Bliss, Washington Gladden and Walter Rauschenbusch.[6] Ransom had been exposed to Strong and Gladden at the World's Parliament of Religion. He also

42

heard Gladden speak at the A.M.E. General Conference in 1900.

Another pivotal figure during the period was the utopian socialist, Edward Bellamy. A committed Christian, Bellamy's novel, Looking Backward, 2000-1887, published in 1888, pictured a commonwealth where socialism had been nonviolently achieved. Bellamy's new world was a fictionalized appropriation of the Christian Socialist Commonwealth, where the means of production and distribution were organized on a cooperative or national basis rather than on a profit motive. Like George and his single-tax scheme, Bellamy's utopian vision became the center of a fairly broad reform movement with the establishment of Nationalist clubs throughout the country.[7] It is probable that Ransom was aware of the voluminous literature addressing the issure of socialism during the 1880's. In any case, Ransom was aware of this issue in the A.M.E. Church and debated its influence within the black community.

During the last two decades of the nineteenth century, the A.M.E. Review periodically addressed socialism, communism and the rights of labor.[8] Howerver, black leaders were generally wary of radical economic solutions, as an 1886 Review article by Alexander Clark on socialism indicates. Even though Clark was aware of racial and economic discrimination against Blacks, he asserted his belief in American capitalsim and its ability to provide individual opportunity for black advancement. He feared communism's goal of abolishing property, its advocacy of total governmental control, and its antipathy toward marriage and the family. These factors were the source of Clark's anxieties, and thus, he described communism as secretive, dangerous, and indecent.[9]

Socialism, in Clark's view, was perceived in a somewhat positive light. It endeavored to obtain for workers a decent wage, a co-partnership between labor and industry, the abolishment of class legislation and the equality of all men under the law. Futhermore, he saw socialism embodied in the Knights of Labor and considered its position closely related the the Christian vision of brotherhood and economic justice. In fact, he acknowledged socialism's attractiveness to the "African-American" populace. Nevertheless, he urged Blacks to keep faith in God and in the American economic system and to refuse involvement in "the plots of

43

anarchists."[10] He called upon his fellows to remember thier historic allegiance to God and country by concluding, "We want nothing of socialism or the commune, the strike or the boycott, the mob or the riot."[11]

Like Clark, most black leaders found the issue of socialism and communism a sensitive one since any association or identification with these radical ideologies jeopardized the precarious situation in which their people lived. Often denied their full citizenship rights, Blacks could ill afford to be labelled un-American, unpatriotic and anarchistic. In addition, these labels could raise the probability of further abuse and increased white violence. Such labels were dangerous ones, since Blacks had been continous victims of violence since slavery. To the extent that socialism and communism advocated revolution and violence of one regime over another, these black leaders felt themselves in no position to make such radical affiliations. This was one of the reasons why very few Blacks embraced socialism as a means of changing their racial condition. However, Ransom was an exception, as were a few of his associates in the Niagara Movement.[12] Ransom argued that the depressions of 1893 and 1896 were the result of man's machinations rather than that of a divinely ordered plan. Thus, by 1896, Ransom was prepared to support one possible solution.

On July 4, 1896, Ransom addressed the Ohio Federation of Labor on "Negro Socialism."[13] From his vantage point, socialism was ushering in a new world order, one that would drastically change the relations between men. He envisioned a new era in which corporations would no longer be able to deny working people a living wage. Ransom's thought paralleled a Christian Socialist position in his idea that all natural resources were given by God and belonged to no one nationalistic group of peoples; rather, these resources were given by the Master for the benefit of the human race.[14] Ransom was also convinced that since the overwhelming majority of Blacks were working-class, they would be attracted to and eventually espouse the cause of socialism. As proletarians, the interests of black and white workers were one. He believed that white workers would not be able to succeed without the support of the black working class. Solidarity would not be achieved if this labor movement sanctioned divisiveness and separatism. Ransom stressed that

44

> The battles of socialism are not to be fought by white men, for the benefit of white men. It is not, we have said, a question of race, it is a question of men....When millions of toilers are degraded, labor is degraded, man is degraded. While one class of toilers is outraged and oppressed, no man is free.[15]

Ransom believed that centuries of social and industrial oppression had uniquely prepared Blacks to join forces with their fellow white workers. This alliance would occur as soon as black people realized that socialism offered them the possibility of achieving the same economic opportunity as Whites. Irrespective of Ransom's optimism, white socialists were not willing to consider black workers as equals.

Racism within the socialist and labor movements was an obstacle to black and white solidarity. Ideologically, socialists believed that class, not race, was the major barrier to human equality. In their view, historic forces which determin society's classes are economic, not racial. In addition to this stance, socialists were victims of their own racial prejudices and fears. Finally, most socialists looked to white workers and Western intellectuals as the creators of the new age. Blacks and other peoples might follow, but white Western civilization was to lead. This made Ransom's call to the socialists for equality of Blacks in all areas of the movement out of the question.[16]

Ransom also had to face the hostility of organized labor toward Blacks. Most labor unionists were European immigrants who shared little in common with Blacks but the similarity of their straitened circumstances. In recognition of the chasm separating Blacks and labor, Ransom offered two resolutions to the 1899 Afro-American Council's Convention in Chicago: that a committee appointed by the Council

> (1)...confer with leaders of organized labor in the United States to impress upon them the mutual benefits that would accrue to laborers regardless of race (and) their overt discrimination be set aside to bring about a spirit of fraternity and cooperation among American workers of

45

> every grade, regardless of race or
> section;
>
> (2) ... meet with the National Labor Bureau
> to lay before it the conditions of Negro
> laborers in the United States (and) to
> keep them informed in regard to the same,
> and to have them (the Council) appoint,
> if possible, a subcommitte to cooperate
> with the national bureau.[17]

Similar to DuBois and other activists within the Afro-American Council, Ransom was keenly aware of the employment dilemmas facing Blacks. Forced out of jobs by immigrant workers, Blacks' efforts to better their economic condition were threatened by both employers and labors union.[18] Therefore, caught between the antagonistic response of labor and industry, Blacks seemed to have little room for manuevering into a better economic position. However, Ransom, like DuBois, was unwilling to accept defeat. He took his stand with those who believed that Blacks had to endeavor, despite white resistance, to build interracial unity.[19]

Ransom's approach was by no means the only strategy advanced regarding the issue. In actual fact, as the following articles in the _Review_ attest, black leaders held conflicting views. Some urged Blacks to join unions, but warned them about joining locals advocating violence. John R. Lynch was not opposed to union membership, but questioned its efficacy if Blacks lost the good will of their idustrial employers. T. McCants Stewart suggested that Blacks should ask for labor and industry cooperation. Even still, James S. Stemons and J.R. Jenifer looked to white Christian employers to respond with Christian charity and love to the workers, and placed their faith in America's rapidly expanding economy and industrial training and education.[20] Whatever their approaches and strategies, these spokesmen and others like them were limited in their efforts to change the dismal situation of their people since the racial assumptions of the day categorized all Blacks as inferior to all Whites. These assumptions were supported in part by interpretations of Charles Darwin's epochal study, _The Origin of the Species_ (1859).

Darwin proposed that through the means of natural selection, stronger organisms survived and weaker organisms perished. While his theory of evolution challenged traditonal religious doctrine concerning the Biblical view of creation and the origin of humankind, its importance for this study lies in the fact that the theory provided to some men new arguments for their old belief in the superiority and inferiority of racial groups. These persons, referred to as Social Darwinists, applied Darwin's theories concerning the natural order to the social order. Social Darwinists believed that certain peoples were destined by heredity to build and to rule the great civilizations of the world, and that they were destined to rule inferior peoples. According to Social Darwinists, the Anglo-Saxon race had been selected by nature (God) to bring Christianity and democracy to the world's less favored races. Thus, imperialism and racism were buttressed by science and theology.[21] This special mission to civilize the world had long been a part of the American mentality, whether in the Puritan's seventeenth century conception of their call to establish a righteous commonwealth or the country's belief in the first half of the nineteenth century in Manifest Destiny. Thus, by the turn of the twentieth century as American began to sujugate and acquire an empire composed primarily of darker peopl abroad, the condition of black Americans worsened. The ideology of white supremacy had triumphed.[22]

The Social Gospel's attitude toward race generally reflected the spirit of the times as it affirmed Anglo-Saxon superiority and the mission to Christianize the world. For example, the Social Gospel leader, Josiah Strong, was a fierce believer in the superiority of the Anglo-Saxon race. His concern about growing evils within urban American was often couched in racist rhetoric. He stated that the immigration of non-Anglo-Saxon Europeans into the cities was responsible for prostitution, gambling, unemployment, pauperism, crime, and slums. He also tied the political corruption of the time to the influence of foreign immigration. His call for church involvement in societal transformation was an attempt to preserve and extend Anglo-Saxon Christian civilization. He suggested that racial inequality was within God's plan for humanity and said that the Almighty was preparing a "better race" to do and complete His will. For Strong, Anglo-Saxon Protestantism was the glue binding the fabric of society.[23]

Few Social Gospel leaders were as blatantly racist

47

as Strong, but most paid little attention to black people or their problems. These religious reformers ultimately believed in self-help and self-advancement where Blacks were concerned, and therefore urged Blacks to educate themselves and to strive to emulate the standards of white civilization. According to Social Gospelers, the problems of Blacks arose basically out of the race's own deficiencies and would be solved by Blacks' own diligence and hard work. It is no wonder that most Social Gospelers were strong supporters of the gradualist self-help program of Booker T. Washington. They consider industrial education to have been the most realistice approach for a backward race.[24]

Ransom and other black militants did not deny black people's late start in civilization's advance or the need for self-help, but rejected the notion that they were by nature predestined to remain in their debased condition. In Ransom's view, the race's condition was due to the unhealthy environment in which it had to live and not to any inborn racial characteristics. The debilitating residue of slavery and continued prejudice within American sociey were the underlying causes of the race's situation. It is evident from the following speech that Ransom felt obligated to refute those voices alleging the biological inferiority of Blacks.

In an address, "Heredity and Environment," delivered at the Literacy Congress in Indianapolis in 1898, Ransom proposed that every human soul on earth was a "new creation fresh from the hnads of God." Heredity, he believed, was important in the realm of physical characteristics, "but the proper observance of hygienic and physiological law largely contradicted such importance."[25] As far as intellect was concerned, Ransom observed that heredity counted for little. Using Homer, Virgil, Shakespeare, Milton, Hugo and Dickens as examples, of genius, Ransom noted that they had produced no comparable intellectual successors in their family lines.[26] Stangely enough, he continued, "children of the Maori in New Zealand and children of the Aboriginies (in Australia) said to be the lowest on the scale of human intelligence, have taken honors from the children of parents who have in back of them centuries of civilization and culture."[27] Citing black men who had taken highest honors at Harvard, Yale, and Michigan State between 1896 and 1898, Ransom noted that they had achieved that distinction "over all the wealth and culture of the boasted Anglo-Saxon intelligence."[28]

Ransom reversed the Social Darwinist preoccupation with heredity and asseted that "environment is the mighty vortex into which we are all caught and our life and character are shaped almost without our will."[29]

According to Ransom, the lowly condition of Blacks was due to environmental circumstances. "Whenever the social atmosphere is depressed and stagnant, it breeds disease and death. It is in light of these things (that) our race should be tried or judged."[30] Since Ransom believed that black personhood and identity came from God, he concluded that Blacks must change their man-made environment and improve the conditions under which they lived.[31] Thus, he did not dispute evolutionary theory, but viewed it as progressive and not static. Similar to other Social Gospeler,[32] Ransom refashioned the theory of evolution to fit his theological framework. He believed that it was black people's God-given duty to struggle for the kind of societal change that allowed them access to employment, education and the franchise. Then and only then would Blacks be free to develop and contribute to the world the distinctive talents and gifts given them by God.

Ransom accepted with some modifications Darwin's theory of evolution, and therefore he did not dispute the prevalent belief in the racial basis of culture. According to this view, certain races were endowed by God to make particular contributions to the world. Ransom developed a theoretical basis for black equality and uniqueness as did other contemporaries like DuBois and Kelly Miller.

In his 1897 essay, "The Conservation of the Races," DuBois argued that the history of the world was the history of races. He divided the races of the world into eight distinct groups, giving to each a particular culture or spirit. He postulated that

> The English nation stood for constitutional liberty and commercial freedom; the Grecian nation for science and philosophy, the Romance nations stood for literature and art, and the other race groups (were) striving, each in its own way, to develop for civilizations its particular message, its particular ideal, which shall help to guide the world nearer and nearer that perfection of human life for which we all long...[33]

DuBois saw the Negro race contributing its music, its compassionate nature, and its inspired poetry to the world.[34]

Kelly Miller confirmed his belief in racial characteristics by adopting evolutionary theory to support his racial analysis. In an essay entitled the "Artistic Gift of the Negro" (1908), he listed six areas in which the black race had made laudable contributions. Miller suggested areas of the fine arts, music, oratory, poetry, painting and literature. Racial development had followed that of the human race. He wrote that "Imaginative process emerges first and exact knowledge and its practical application comes at a later stage."[35]

Like DuBois and Miller, Ransom also theorized about the racial characteristics of particular groups; races like individuals were endowed differently, whether spiritually or physically. In a sermon entitled "Race Soil," delivered in 1894 to the youth of St. John's A.M.E. Church, Ransom mentioned several races and their contributions to the world: the Jewish contribution had been moral and spiritual, the Greeks had given the world its culture, and the Romans had gifted humanity with its law.[36] He challenged the young people to take advantage of their disadvantages, reminding them that the future was before them. Unlike the older races whose special endowments and distinctive qualities had been exhausted, black people were on the verge of their racial development and productivity. Describing to the youth what DuBois wrote in 1897 and Miller essentially outlined in 1908, although with a decidedly religious emphasis, Ransom stated:

> ...We believe that with his natural music talent, the Negro will cause sweeter harmonies and pretty melodies to waft in the air than ever enraptured the human soul. Eloquent of speech, he will plead the cause of God and the welfare of mankind with such tones of power that neither rostrum nor the forum ever heard. His deep emotional nature will be the foe of tyranny and oppression and as a religious vehicle will carry the triumph of the King of Kings into the seats of pride and power, and over the dark and barren regions of the globe.[37]

Thus, Ransom's sermon demonstrates clearly that

Ransom, Miller and DuBois were products of their times. Neither of them denied the assumption that racial groups possessed distinctive characteristics and traits. Moreover, they attempted to formulate and disseminate a basic defense of the racial characteristics of Blacks. However, Random did vehemently reject the contention made by the American church that it was destined, through its Anglo-Saxon heritage, to Christianize the world. It is important to note that Ransom did not disavow the concept of a Christian mission, but rather proposed another instrumentality for its expression. Ransom contended that the black church and black people were the world's best hope to realize God's world-wide Kingdom of social and racial justice. Since white Protestantism refused to condemn America's racism at home and supported its imperialistic adventures abroad, Ransom concluded that the white church had forfeited its mission to be God's herald in the world.

In a sermon delivered in 1896, Ransom made the connection between the plight of Blacks in Africa, the West Indies and in America and the policies of the United States government. Blacks shared a common dilemma and a common destiny, he said.[38] He called upon American Blacks to join forces with Africa and the West Indies in their common struggle for rights. Ransom excoriated white churches for proclaiming brotherhood while countenancing racial discrimination and reminded Blacks that they had a mission "to take their stand against American Christianity" and its racial hyprocrisy.[39] In 1912, Ransom noted what he called the "colonization and exploitation of the backward peoples of the earth, and the colonial policy of this (United States) democratic republic in dealing with Hawaii, Puerto Rico and the Philippines. Since the white church remained silent about those injustices, it was the responsibility of the black church to speak out against them.[40]

In 1920, describing Anglo-Saxon civilization as brutal and possessing an insatiable lust and greed for power, Ransom accused American Christianity of aiding and abetting its expansionistic policy. He asserted that the Cross of Christ had preceded the enemy in its subjugation of dark-skinned people and the seizure of their resources. Ransom was no doubt in agreement with Edwin Smith who indicated that "the motive underlying the partition of Africa by Europeans was guided one-tenth by civilizing zeal and nine-tenths by the bait of gain."[41] For this reason, Ransom was certain that the moral bankruptcy of American Christianity endangered Africa's very soul. In his mind, the black race was the "last reserve of the world's races capable of establishing the Supremacy of Human Unity, Equality and Concord."[42] Ransom looked to Americans of African descent "to keep Africans from being damned by that form of salvation known as Christian civilization." Ransom's concept of the spirituality of Africans and their black descendants was derived from his belief in the unique racial endowments of peoples. He categorized Whites as possessing cognitive and rational faculties, while postulating that Blacks possessed intuitive and emotional faculties. He constantly expressed the belief that black people not only had a "richer and deeper emotional endowment," but that they were friendlier and kinder than white people.[43]

Ransom also believed that Blacks possessed the racial trait of cheerfulness and goodwill in addition to a natural inclination towards things of the spirit and of the heart. Addressing the Annual Convocation of the Howard Univeristy School of Religion in 1925 on the subject, "The Spiritual Leaderhsip of the Negro Ministry," Ransom clearly revealed his belief in the special mission of black America to the world. Using Mahatma Gandhi as an example of one who was aware of his destiny, Ransom urged the ministers gathered at the School of Religion to apprehend the missions to which they had been called.

He acknowledged the outstanding achievements of white men in the material and physical worlds and cautioned his listeners not to attempt to compete with them in that realm. However, he felt it was absolutely essential that the Howard seminarians recognize that they had been chosen to make more valuable contributions to the world in the realm of the human spirit. "We have scarcely scratched the surface of the things that relate to the out-givings of the heart from man to man, much less the deeper things of the human soul. Spiritual leadership can only come from a spiritual people."[44] In Ransom's view, a vacuous, depleted, and essentially unchristian American Christianity desperately needed the spiritual contribution only black people could give.

Furthermore, he urged the ministers gathered at the School of Religion to seriously consider the prospect that the church they were preparing to serve required daring and innovative leaders. With urbanization and the enormous increase of southern Blacks migrating to the cities, they had to devise new ministerial approaches if the church was to survive. Ransom spoke from the perspective of one who had twenty-five years earlier created such a new approach as the Institutional Church and Social Settlement. It must be remembered that the Social Gospel Movement intentionally sought to prod the church into redefining its function and meaning in the modern world. The struggle over that definition within white and black churches was a long and bitter one.

Carter G. Woodson described the struggle for direction within the black church as a battle between "conservative and progressive" forces. What the church was to be and how it was to function in the changing times was the overriding question.[45] DuBois described two distinct leadership groups representing divergent ethical viewpoints within the black church: the latter group, influenced by modern ideas, was just about ready to reject traditional religion and "curse God", while the other, committed to the old-time religion, continued its ties to "remote and whimsical" ideals. DuBois noted that the great mass of black people wavered between the two contending groups, one having "lost the guiding star of the past" and the other seeking out of the tumultuous times "a new religious ideal." Like its white counterpart, the black church was searching to find its way through a period of enormous change.[46]

Ransom, while consistently aligned with the "progressives," did not "curse God." He endeavored to bridge the gap that divided the proponents of the "old and new" by advocating a church and ministry with the old values, yet equipped with the necessary knowledge and insight to impart the old-time religion in ways relevant to new circumstances and times. He believed that the survival of the church hinged upon its ability to meet the needs of its people in an increasingly complex world and time.

As the nineteenth century ended, few, if any, denied the pivotal role played by the church in the history of black America. According to DuBois, a most trenchant and sometimes caustic critic, the black church antedated the black family in America and preserved many functions of African tribal organization as well as many functions of the family.[47] In his study, The

Philadelphia Negro, DuBois proposed six well-defined functions of the church in black life in the late 1890's: the raising of the annual budget, the maintenance of membership, social intercourse and assessments, the setting of moral standards, promotion of general intelligence, and efforts for social betterment.[48]

A decade and a half after DuBois' study, Richard R. Wright, in The Negro in Pennsylvania: A Study in Economic History, concluded that the black church was still the chief social institution in the black community. It provided welcome and aid to strangers, particularly immigrants from the South. It aided and encouraged concerts, lectures and other entertainments, allowing its facilities to be used as a meeting place for groups, clubs, fraternal organizations and civic associations of every kind.[49] Similarly, Ransom saw black people seeking the fulfillment of their aspirations within the church , having "made it the medium of expression, not only of (their) religions, but of (their) secular life as well."[50]

Thus, Ransom believed that the black church was obligated to teach its people, not only health and cleanliness, decorum and ordr, and how to pray, but what to pray for. It was the teaching function of the church to open the eyes of its congregants to their relationship to God and their redemptive partnership with Christ in the salvation of the world. We have here in brief a central facet of Ransom's understanding of the church's task. It was to nurture, develop, and equip black people, morally, spiritually and intellectually, to change a racist society into one in which justice and brotherhood prevailed. The black church, therefore, was the "mother institution" from which the family, higher education, and individual as well as group leadership had been conceived.[51] Yet, despite the accomplishments of the past, Ransom realized that the church faced difficult challenges in 1900. His perspective was informed by the experiences of his previous urban pastorates.

Despite the problem caused by urbanization and industrialization, Ransom found city life exciting and exhilarating and believed that northern cities provided more possibilities for Blacks than did life in the South,[52] and thereby supported efforts encouragaing Blacks to migrate North. This viewpoint had its

54

detractors, however, for A.M.E. Bishop L.J. Coppin deplored the migration of Blacks from the South to the North. He found, as did many other black and white protestants of the day, the lure of the city to be dangerous and ultimately destructive of those values existing in small-town America. The city, according to Coppin, was a place of temptations for black youth, where unrestrained immoralities flourished. The arrival of large numbers of Blacks from a way of life they understood to an unknown world in the North could only bring disaster. The Bishop encouraged Blacks to acquire land for farming. Noting that young people the world over appeared to be leaving the country for the city, Coppin hoped that a remedy might be found to halt the movement from "the farm to the factories."[53] Other prominent voices within the community urged Blacks to remain in the South. According to this view, opportunities for black advancement were better in the South, since northern discrimination prohibited their employment in most trades and professions.[54]

Ransom was not deterred by those difficulties, but urged the church to broaden its mission in order to adequately respond to the new immigrants. During the 1890's, when the migration of Blacks from the South to the North was but a trickle compared to the flood during and immediately following World War I. Ransom experienced the bewilderment of the church in its inability to cope with the problems that the early migration caused. He remembered that in Chicago the black clergy "were unprepared by training, experience and vision to cope with the moral, social and economic conditions so suddenly thrust upon them."[55]

The numerous programs and activities he initiated at Bethel and Institutional Churches were organized to meet some of the needs of the arriving migrants. Ransom's concern was to broaden the concept of the church as an active participant in the total life of its community.

He realized that the demands upon the church to broaden its functions would increase dramatically as the number of migrants swelled. He anticipated that the migrants would have adjustment problems and urged the black church to give attention to their "social, moral and spiritual welfare." Ransom saw an opportunity for large black denominations, Methodists and Baptist, to make their southern brethren "realize the full measure

55

of American opportunity and manhood."[56]

Ransom was sharply critical of the church's limited response to the migrants and he accused churches of responding to their presence in traditionally narrow denominational ways. He said that by concentrating upon their own ecclesiastical concerns, the bishops of the three major black Methodist denominations were allowing the opportunities for service to evade them. Instead, other agencies, such as the YWCA and YMCA were responding to the needs of the migrants.[57] To enable the church to respond to the needs of people, Ransom urged the bishops to coordinate their urban programs.

Ransom advocated the creation of new administrative structures within the denominations. He proposed in 1920 that fifty percent of the monies normally raised for administrative purposes in five Episcopal Districts be allocated to the missionary Secretary of the church to provide new meeting houses and places of worship for the migrants. Such funds would also be used to support those persons sent to serve the migrants. Ransom doubted that the organized churches already existing in large urban centers would be able to accomplish much in dealing with the newcomers. He noted, "What is needed is to plant the church in the midst of the people where they are."[58] Ransom urged various autonomous departments within the A.M.E. Church to cooperate and outline a comprehensive and cohesive program in response to the migration. Further, he recommended that capable persons be hired to ascertain the actual condition of black people and report their findings to the church for discussion and programmatic action. People best served God "not so much by their presence at the church as by their presence in the crowded communities and around the industrial plant where our men, women and children live and work."[59] Unfortunately, Ransom's recommendations were unheeded.

Ransom believed that the migration presented the A.M.E. Church and other black denominations the opportunity for cooperative Christian service. Once again, Ransom saw an opportunity for the churches to unify on behalf of the race's salvation. In the past, color, class, and differing social and political strategies within the black community had thwarted joint action. He pleaded with all who could hear to "look beyond the boundaries of your Episcopal District, look beyond the boundaries of your denomination and behold the crying needs of your people and your opportunities for cooperation in the work of the Kingdom of God."[60] Ransom's call for inter-denominational cooperation among black churches was yet another example of the Social Gospel's influence in his thought and action.

Many early proponents of Christian unity and inter-church cooperation were Social Gospelers.[61] These leaders were convinced that the problems facing society and religion required the concerted action of the churches in ways that denominationalism impeded. Moreover, men such as Gladden and especially Ransom, often chafed under the institutional and theological restrictions imposed by their more conservative fellow religionists. Although highly articulate, and sometimes influential within their denominations, Social Gospelers were never more than a minority within American Protestantism. They sought to establish a religious movement that transcended the barriers of doctrine, polity and tradition. The Social Gospel emphasized the application of Christian principles to the conditions of people's lives. Ransom expressed similar views in his inaugural address as editor of the A.M.E. Review.

He said that the religious press was not so much concerned about a person's doctrinal beliefs as it was about the quality and worth of his service. He proposed that Review articles and editorials encourage fraternity and cooperation among Christian. While the purpose and task of the religious press was to bear witness to the unity of God's world, no person, whether Jew or Gentile, rich or poor, black or white, was to be excluded from God's concern.[62] The nondenominational cast of Instiutional Church was an expression of Ransom's ecumenical commitment. His exposure to and participation in national and international church meetings undoubtedly accounts for the catholicity of his vision. These events had a specific impact on his intellectual development.

The World Parliament of Religion in 1893 was probably Ransom's first exposure to ecumenical religion; however, it would not be his last. In 1896, he travelled to San Francisco as a delegate to the General Convention of the United Society of Christian Endeavor. Accompanied by Benjamin W. Arnett and sixteen other A.M.E. Delegates, Ransom attended the Third Ecumenical Conference of Methodism held in London in 1901. Methodists from around the globe gathered to discuss temperance, Sunday Schools, the world-wide mission work of the church and spiritual unity.[63] In an address entitled "Work of the Methodist Church in the Twentieth Century," delivered at the London Conference, Ransom challenged his fellow delegates to continue their commitment to the "common people." Methodism, he said, was historically the church of the "masses" and the migration of people, especially the young, from the country to the cities offered the church a splendid opportunity to continue its historic commitment to Christian education. Recognizing the church's long-standing support of higher education, Ransom urged his listeners not to neglect the many young souls residing in the urban centers of the world. Unlike the nineteenth century church, Ransom envisioned a twentieth century church constructed to serve as the central educative and uplifting influence in people's life development. Referring to his own experience at the Institutional Church in Chicago, he saw the emergence of churches open seven days a week, ministering to the toal community in which they were located. He believed that the major task before the churches was the formation of the young into boys and girls of Christian character and integrity. If the cities were to be saved, they required a morally trained and enlightened citizenry. The Social Gospel's concern about urbanization, its emphasis on social and individual regeneration and its tendency to identify Christian influence with democratic practice is clearly represented in that speech.[64]

Settings such as the World Parliament of Religion and the Ecumencial Conference of Methodism offered their participants an opportunity to receive and share their experiences of social Christianity. Ransom found their deliberations immensely important, representing the A.M.E. Church at the Ecumenical Conferences in Toronto in 1911, in London in 1921, and in Springfield, Massachuesetts in 1947.[65] In a 1921 Review editorial, Ransom responded to those who criticized the expenditure of funds for the 1921 meeting. Using the 1901 Methodist meeting in London as an example, he maintained that "A progressive church must be involved in the national and international movements that make for Christian cooperation."[66] He also recalled the 1893 Parliament of Religion meeting in Chicago and the outstanding contributions that were made by Frederick Douglass and Benjamin W. Arnett. Their presence, he concluded, could not be valued monetarily because they had battled those forces attempting to use political science, science and religion to justify their treatment of people on the basis of color and race. He believed that the critical times in which Blacks lived required the A.M.E. Church to be represented at national and international religious gatherings where great issues affecting the world community were debated and discussed.[67] Ransom's involvement in the Federal Council of Churches of Christ in America testified to his commitment to ecumenicity and interdenominational coooperation. Organized in 1908, the Federal Council of the Churches of Christ in America was the culminating achievement of the Social Gospel Movement.

Social Gospelers had contended that the problems of modern life could not be addressed without unified Christian action. The church's recognition of its responsibility to speak as one voice regarding the social, political and economic issues of the times was one of the important factors that brought the Federal Council into existence. Ransom was an early A.M.E. representative to the Federal Council, and an active member of the Council for many years. He attended his last annual meeting in 1948. Ransom served on the Council's executive committee and chaired its Race Relations Commission. He served in the latter capacity with his friend and co-worker, Dr. George E. Haynes, who was the staff director of the Race Relations Commission.

While it is difficult to specifically document the reasons why Ransom supported the Council over the years, it is reasonable to assume that one of the reasons involved his conviction that the black church needed to be represented in an organization of the Council's significance. More importantly, Ransom hoped that the Council would be Christendom's voice for racial justice. In a 1917 Review editorial, Ransom considered the Federal Council to be the best and most effective organization of "social redemption" within Protestant America. However, the Council was primarily interested in redeeming industrial America from the conflicts engendered by capital and labor, and the issue of race was not high on its agenda of concerns. Thus, despite its ringing declaration affirming racial justice, the Council avoided implementing the declaration's content in its member churches or in the general society. Ransom's description of one Council session is illustrative of the racial situation in America during the Council's first decade. At that particular Council meeting, during the presentation of a report by the Committee on Special Interests of Colored Denominations, a white minister from Texas arose to condone lynching as a means of protecting white women of the South. Ransom wrote that the Texan and other delegates were particularly incensed by a paragraph within the report which read:

> There is also among the Negroes an increasing distrust of the white race, and a growing contempt for its religion and its sense of justice--feelings which are breeding a new spirit of antagonism and aggression. And through all this tangle of suspicion and hatred, in this professedly Christian land, mob violence stalks unimpeded, deepening the Negro's distrust, and inflaming the worst passions of lawless Whites.[68]

Ransom may have participated in the writing of that report and if not, the report most certainly reflected his point of view. The black council delegates were asked to delete the objectionable paragraphs which they consented to do, according to Ransom, in "the interest of peace and harmony." Another paragraph considerably more moderte in tone was approved. It stated that Lynch law was no cure for the end of crime, but rather aggravated crime, weakened the law, and if unchecked, could retard progress and destroy civilization." Ransom said, "It did not satisfy radicals like myself and others, but we realized that we were living in the United States and not in the mellenium" (sic).[69] Considering the immense distance between the Council and the nation's creeds and deeds, Ransom looked toward the unification of the black Methodist denominations and black churches to usher in the new age.[70]

Union between black Methodists had been discussed as early as 1820. The attempt at merger between the Allenites (A.M.E.s) and the Zionites (A.M.E.Z.s) was unsuccessful.[71] The two bodies did not resume negotiations until 1846, and afterwards continued to meet toward organic union in 1864, 1868, 1885 ad 1892. Segments within the two denominations and opinion throughout the national black community felt that race advancement would be enhanced by their unification. However, there were numerous reasons why merger was difficult to achieve. Questions of church government, how and for what terms bishops were to be elected, and what the unified chuch would be called were the major impediments to merger. However, the great obstacle to union was the issue of power. Aspirants for the Bishopric in both churches opposed the merger, fearing that their chances for Episcopal election in a united church wuld be lessened. The aspirants were succeful in their opposition,[72] and the attempts at merger failed. Even so, Booker T. Washington, in a commencement address delivered to the Wilberforce University class of 1906, challenged the A.M.E.s, A.M.E.Z.s and the C.M.E.s (the Colored Methodist Episcopal Church founded out of the Methodist Episcopal Church, South in 1870) to unite for the good of Christendom and the race.[73]

In the first issue as editor of the Review (July 1912), Ransom declared his support for the eventual union of the black Methodist denominations. He suggested that a first step toward federation might involve weaker churches (those small in members and in financial recources) agreeing to merge with larger and more financially able churches. Such actions would not only prevent communities from being over-churched, but also discourage the inter-church rivalries and conflicts arising when too many churches compete for too few members. Finally, he said, the financial burden of the people would be lightened.[74] Ransom believed that a united black Methodism would be a powerful agent in the struggle for racial and social change. He longed for the day when the energies and resources so often dissipated in needless rivalry and competition would be used to advance the interests of black people. Thus, religious unification as a means to fight for black rights was uppermost in Ransom's mind.

For that reason, when the Councils of Bishops representing their respective denomination met in Birmingham, Alabama in 1918 and voted to consider orgranic union under the name The United Methodist Episcopal Church, Ransom warned his church to consider seriously its vote. He was less than sanguine about the willingness and ability of the C.M.E. Church to wage the battle for manhood rights in the spirit of the A.M.E. Church because of C.M.E.'s financial dependence upon the Methodist Episcopal Church, South. The A.M.E.Z. Church, on the other hand, was closer to the A.M.E.s in the racial struggle, but continued to have an institutional apparatus different from the A.M.E.'s. Above all,

Ransom stressed that denominational and doctrinal considerations notwithstanding, the three branches of Methodism should be one in their convictions about the role black people should play in society. Ransom expressed this concern unequivocally when he said, "If these bodies cannot unite to fight to a finish the great battle for racial equality and manhood which the A.M.E. Church has been waging for a hundred years, far better now that each should keep its separate path, uniting at all points where cooperation is possible."[75] Although Ransom felt his position was misunderstood and unjustifiably criticized by the proponents or unification, he was convinced that differences between the A.M.E.s and the other Methodist denominations had to be exposed if real and effective union was to occur.

Reporting about the 1920 A.M.E. General Conference in the pages of the Review, Ransom expressed the thrill of seeing men sing, laugh, cry and shout for joy when they heard that the three church bodies of independent Methodists had voted for organic union. He was now persuaded that the three denominations were sufficiently prepared to accomplish the task of racial uplift. The proposal for union was sent to their Annual Conferences for approval,[76] but in April, 1922, the plan was defeated. Ransom lamented the heritage of suspicion, the lure of ambition, and the intransigency of authority and power that had defeated the plan. Attempts to revive the talks occured during the next quarter centruy and Ransom continued to be involved in those efforts. As late as 1949, Ransom urged the A.M.E. and A.M.E.Z. denominations to appoint a preliminary committee to discuss union. Describing denominational schism as "the plague of world Protestant Christianity," Ransom warned that failure to unify would hasten the declining influence of the church.[77]

Thus, recognizing the difficulties unification entailed, Ransom, along with others, founded in 1934 the Fraternal Council of Negro Churches. He was elected its first president. Patterned after the Federal Council of Churches, the Fraternal Council consisted of twelve black denominations, representing seven million members: The A.M.E., A.M.E.Z., and C.M.E. churches, the Central Jurisdiction (black) of the Methodist Church, the two leading black Baptist conventions, the African Orthodox Church, the Freewill Baptist, the Church of God in Christ, the Apostolic Churches, the Bible Way Church of Washington, D.C., the Church of God in Christ, the

Church of God and Saints of Christ, and the Metropolitan Community Church of Chicago.[78] Each denomination was represented by delegates, but at Fraternal Council's meetings, the denominations were not bound by Fraternal Council actions. The Fraternal Council was Ransom's way of creating a platform from which black Christendom could address contemporary issues. It was the Social Gospel from the black perspective asserting, as it did in the church, its right to voice the concerns of black people in the United States. The Fraternal Council of Negro Churches was Ransom's attempt to unify and strengthen the black church in the struggle for racial and social justice. He believed that the very existence of the church depended upon its ability to offer to black people hope and encouragement in difficult times. The Council's public message which was issued during the height of the Depression is illustrative of Ransom's concern:

> If the Negro church is to survive, it must offer the Negro youth of today something more than a home in heaven. Faced with the attitude of American Chrisitanity, American business, labor, industry and the govenrment itself, who shall give the Faith, Hope, and Courage to persevere? The righteousness of God, the life and teachings of Jesus Christ, must be relied upon to survive the wreckage of racial antagonism and legal and social injustice, oppression, and denial.[79]

Unfortunately, the constitutional nature of the Fraternal Council doomed it to failure, for none of its constituent members were willing to underwrite its activities or be bound by its resolutions. The Fraternal Council met in national convention from 1934 to 1939 but no meetings were held in 1940 and 1941. In 1942, Ransom sent a memorandum to all persons who had been members or were interested in reoranizing efforts the Fraternal Council.[80] Although successful in its reorganizing efforts, the Council was never the influence Ransom had hoped. He and its other leaders lacked the time and energy to give to the Council, and the organization was bereft of the finances necessary to develop a staff and apparatus to communicate and implement its message and program. The Fraternal Council of Negro Churches is representative of an effort led by Ransom and other activist to awaken black churches and black denominations to the social implications of the faith, while the Council's demise is some indication that Ransom failed in his efforts to unite black Christendom in the struggle for racial and social change.

Thus, it is important to consider that the ideas and concepts Ransom used and refashioned were not intended as knowledge for knowledge sake, however laudatory that endeavor. Essentially, Ransom was always concerned abouth the practical applicability of ideas in the world. Ransom was foremost a man of action, and his life and ministry consistently combined theory and practice, thought and action, and word and deed. As has been said of another clergyman, Ransom's"...genius lay in his ability to synthesize creatively from a variety of sources and to interpret comples issues in ways that non-theologians could understand (and use)."[81]

Lastly, Ransom's intellectual curiosity and his quest for knowledge must be considered if the developmental process shaping him is to be understood. He is said to have read every available theological book at Wilberforce by the time of his graduation. Ever alert to the stirrings within America, Ransom kept abreast of the new writings in science, political science, sociology, economics and Biblical criticism. Thus, Ransom did not appear on America's racial, social and theological scene indifferent to the broader intellectual currents of his times.

Footnotes

[1] Reverdy C. Ransom, "Editoral, The New Emancipation," A.M.E. Review, January 1913, pp. 260-61.

[2] Hopkins, The Rise of the Social Gospel, pp. 3-7, 172.

[3] Hopkins, The Rise of the Social Gospel, pp. 171-83.

[4] Abell, The Urban Impact, pp. 78-81. especially p. 79; May, Protestant Churches, pp. 249-56; Hopkins, The Rise of the Social Gospel, pp. 184-200.

[5] Library of Reverdy C. Ransom, Tawawa Chimney Corners, Wilberforce, Ohio.

[6] Hopkins, The Rise of the Social Gospel, pp. 59-60; May, Protestant Churches, p. 154-56; Abell, Urban Impact, pp. 67-68.

[7] May, Protestant Churches, pp. 157-58; Hopkins, The Rise of the Social Gospel, pp. 173-74.

[9] Clark, "Socialism," A.M.E. Review, July, 1886, pp. 53, 50; Philip S. Foner, American Socialism and Black Americans (Westport, Connecticut; Greenwood Press, 1977), pp. 84-85.

[10] Clark, "Socialism," A.M.E. Review, pp. 50, 53-54.

[11] Clark, "Socialism," A.M.E. Review, p. 54.

[12] Meier, Negro Thought, pp. 185, 189; Gerber, Black Ohio, pp. 175-76.

[13] Gazette, July 4, 1896.

[14] Ransom, "The Negro and Socialism," A.M.E. Review, October, 1896, pp. 192, 196-97.

[15] Ransom, "The Negro and Socialism," A.M.E. Review, pp. 197-98, 200; "The Industrial and Social Condition of the Negro," Ransom Papers, Payne Theological Seminary; Meier, Negro Thought, p. 185; Jervis Anderson, A. Philip Randolph (New York: Harcourt Brace, Jovanovich, Inc. 1972,), p. 72.

[16]H. Wayne Morgan, ed., American Socialism, 1900-1960 (Englewood Cliffs, New Jersey: Prentice Hall, Inc., 1964), pp. 71-72; Robert L. Allen, Reluctant Reformers: Racism and Social Reform Movements in the United States (New York: Anchor Books, 1975), pp. 226-27; Foner, American Socialism and Black Americans, p. xiii.

[17]"Afro-American Council Meeting," Chicago Journal, August 18, 1899.

[18]DuBois, Philadelphia Negro, pp. 110-16, 126-30; Ransom, "The Industrial and Social Conditions of the Negro," pp. 7-9.

[19]Philip S. Foner, Organized Labor and the Black Worker, 1619-1973 (New York: International Publishers, 1976), p. 80.

[20]John R. Lynch, "Should Colored Men Join Labor Organization?" A.M.E. Review, October, 1886, pp. 165-67; T. McCants Stewart, "The Afro-American As a Factor in the Labor Problem," A.M.E. Review, July, 1889, p. 36; James Samuel Stemons, "The Industrial Color Line in the North and the Remedy," A.M.E. Review, January, 1896, pp. 346-56; J.T. Jenifer, "The Labor Question, North and South," A.M.E. Review, April, 1897, pp. 371-74.

[21]Richard Hofstader, Social Darwinism in American Thought (Boston: Beacon Press, 1955), pp. 170-200; Thomas F. Gossett, Race: The History of An Idea in America (new York: Schocken Books, 1965), pp. 144-75; George M. Frederickson, The Black Image in the White Mind (New York: Harper Torchbooks, 1972), pp. 228-55; Allen, Reluctant Reformers, pp. 88-91.

[22]Allen, Reluctant Reformers, p. 91.

[23]William G. P. Bliss, The Encylopedia of Social Reform (New York: Funk & Wagnalls Co., 1897), pp. 289-90, 109-10, 711-15; Robert T. Handy, A Christian America (New York: Oxford University Press, 1971), pp. 179-80; Gossett, Race: The History of An Idea in America, pp. 178, 185-93.

[24]Handy, A Christian America, pp. 174-81.

[25]Ransom, The Spirit of Freedom and Justice, p. 161.

[26] Ransom, The Spirit of Freedom and Justice, pp. 161-62. Ransom returned to this theme in his autobiography, stating that children raised in the Wilberforce community, the progeny of professors and bishops, rarely attained the intellectual eminence of their parents. Writing perhaps about himself, he said, "It is the children who have come from afar, with a thirst for knowledge, who have gone beyond them in achievement, distinction and honor." Pilgrimage, pp. 40-41.

[27] Ransom, The Spirit of Freedom and Justice, p. 162.

[28] Ransom, The Spirit of Freedom and Justice, p. 162.

[29] Ransom, The Spirit of Freedom and Justice, p. 162.

[30] Ransom, Disadvantages and Opportunities, pp. 8-9.

[31] Ransom, The Spirit of Freedom and Justice, p. 163.

[32] Hopkins, The Rise of the Social Gospel, pp. 149-53.

[33] W.E.B. DuBois, "The Conservation of Races," in Howard Brotz, ed., Negro Social and Political Thought, 1850-1920, (New York: Basic Books, Inc., Publishers, 1966), p. 487.

[34] Brotz, Negro Social and Political Thought, 1850-1920, pp. 489, 491.

[35] Kelly Miller, Radicals and Conservatives (New York: Schocken Books, 1968), pp. 255-56.

[36] Ransom, Disadvantages and Opportunities, pp. 6-8.

[37] Ransom, Disadvantages and Opportunities, p. 13.

[38] Ransom, "The Industrial and Social Conditions of the Negro," A Thanksgiving Sermon delivered at Bethel A.M.E. Church, Chicago, November 26, 1896, p. 13. Ransom Papers, Wilberforce University Archives.

[39] Ransom, "The Industrial and Social Conditions of the Negro," pp. 13-14.

[40] Ransom, The Spirit of Freedom and Justice, p. 92.

[41] Ransom, "Editorial, The Kaiser and the Yellow Peril Now Yield to the Red Menace of Bolshevism," A.M.E. Review (October, 1920), pp. 86-87; Edwin Smith, The Golden Stool (London: Holborn Publishing House, 1927), p. 25.

[42] Ransom, "The Coming Vision," A.M.E. Review (January, 1921), p. 139; "Editorial, Africa, and the Americans of African Descent," A.M.E. Review (April, 1922), pp. 201-2.

[43] Ransom, The Negro, Hope or Despair of Christianity, pp. 6-7; Preface to History of A.M.E. Church, pp. 206-7.

[44] Ransom. "The Spiritual Leadership of the Negro Ministry," A.M.E. Review (January, 1925), pp. 112, 110; Reverdy C. Ransom to W.E.B. DuBois, July 2, 1935. DuBois papers, University of Massachusetts.

[45] Woodson, The History of the Negro Church, pp. 224ff.

[46] W.E.B. DuBois, The Souls of Black Folk (New York: McClure & Co., 1903), pp. 149-51.

[47] W.E.B. DuBois, The Souls of Black Folk (New York: McClure & Co., 1903), p. 146; The Philadelphia Negro (New York: Schocken Books, 1967), p. 201.

[48] W.E.B. DuBois, The Philadelphia Negro, pp. 202-7.

[49] R. R. Wright, Jr. The Negro of Pennsylvania: A Study in Economic History (New York: Arno Press & New York Times, 1968), p. 117.

[50] Ransom, "Editorial, The Influence of the Church on the Development and Progress of the American Negro," A.M.E. Review (April, 1918); Ransom and J.W. Robinson, ed., Yearbook of Negro Churches, 1939-40 (Philadelphia: A.M.E. Book Concern, 1939-40), p. 8.

[51]Ransom, "Editorial, The Teaching Church," A.M.E. Review (April, 1922), p. 198.

[52]According to Ransom, the migrants could expect: (1) higher wages and exhorbitant rents; (2) race prejudice and discrimination tending to increase as their numbers grew in any given community; (3) essential public school access for their children; (4) no Jim Crow on public carriers, as a rule equal justice in the courts; (5) protection for their property and themselves; (6) the right to vote. Ransom, "Editorial, The Negro in the North," A.M.E. Review (January, 1917), pp. 151-52.

[53]Levi J. Coppin, "The Thorn in the Flesh - What the Remedy," A.M.E. Review (January, 1910), pp. 262-67; R.R. Wright, Jr. Bishops, pp. 146-50.

[54]Booker T. Washington, etc., The Negro Problem (New York: Arno Press and the New York Times, 1969), pp. 9-29; Miller, Radicals and Conservatives, pp. 133-46; Washington's Industrial Education program which encouraged Blacks to remain in the South was ironically obsolete, even as he advocated it, for industrialization was altering the North and South. Northern industries needed additional workers while southern agriculture required fewer workers.

[55]Ransom, Pilgrimage, p. 82. Between 1890 and 1900, the number of southern-born Blacks residing in Chicago increased from 57,028 to 85,078. U.S. Bureau of Census, Negro Population, 1790-1910, pp. 43-44, 68.

[56]Ransom, "Editorial, The Negro in the North," A.M.E. Review, January, 1917.

[57]Ransom was also aware that the demands of the times required innovative training in order to prepare black seminarians for urban ministry. See his "Editorial, A Call to the Ministry," A.M.E. Review (April, 1920), p. 506.

[58]Ransom, "Editorial, The Church and the Exodus," A.M.E. Review (July, 1917), p. 34.

[59]Ransom, "Editorial, The Church and the Exodus," A.M.E. Review, p. 35.

[60]Ransom, "Editorial, Interdenominational Duty and

Opportunity, <u>A.M.E. Review</u> (January, 1918), p. 176.

[61]May, <u>Protestant Churches</u>, pp. 193-94; Handy, <u>The Social Gospel</u>, pp. 12-13.

[62]Ransom, <u>The Spirit of Freedom and Justice</u>, pp. 91-92.

[63]<u>The Ecumenical Budget of the A.M.E. Church</u>, 1901, p. 55; Ransom Papers, W.S. Smith, <u>History of the A.M.E. Church</u>, p. 224; <u>Minutes of Twenty Second General Conference</u>, 1904 Quadrennial Bishops' Addresses, pp. 4-5.

[64]Ransom, "Work of the Methodist Church in the Twentieth Century," <u>A.M.E. Review</u> (October, 1901), pp. 152-53.

[66]Ransom, "Editorial, The Ecumenical Conference of Methodism" <u>A.M.E. Reivew</u> (October, 1921), pp. 86-87.

[67]Ransom, "Editorial, The Ecumenical Conference of Methodism," p. 87.

[68]Wright, <u>Bishops of the A.M.E. Church</u>, p. 290.

[69]Ransom, "Editorial, The Federal Council," <u>A.M.E. Review</u> (January, 1917), pp. 159-61.

[70]Ransom, "Editorial, Hear What the Spirit Saith Unto the Churches," <u>A.M.E. Reviw</u> (July, 1917), pp. 31-32. An issue later, Ransom printed the ringing declaration of the Council on race. Unfortunately, its words did not become actions. "Hear What the Spirit Saith Unto the Churches," <u>A.M.E. Review</u> (October, 1917), pp. 107-8.

[71]For an analysis of these 1820 merger discussions, see Carol V.R. George, <u>Segregated Sabbath: Richard Allen and the Rise of Independent Black Churches</u>, 1840-1860 (New York: Oxford University Press, 1973), pp. 98-100.

[72]For an extended discussion of those attempts at unification, see Smith, <u>History of the A.M.E. Church</u>, pp. 373-93; Charles S. Butcher, "A Historical Study of Efforts to Secure Church Union Among Independent Negro Methodists (B.D. These, Howard University, School of Religion, 1939), pp. 1-44.

[73]Butcher, "Efforts to Secure Church Union," p. 40.

[74]Ransom, "Editorial, A Step Toward Denominational Union," A.M.E. Review (July, 1912), p. 85.

[75]Butcher, "Efforts to Secure Church Union," pp. 43-44; Smith, History of the A.M.E. Church, p. 391; Ransom, "Editorial, Has the A.M.E. Church Forgotten Its Mission?" A.M.E. Review (October, 1919), pp. 368-69.

[76]Ransom, "Editorial, Organic Union," A.M.E. Review (January, 1921), pp. 155-56; "Editorial, The General Conference of 1920," p. 37.

[77]Ransom, "One Fold One Shepherd, The United Methodist Episcopal Church," Ransom Papers, Wilberforce University Archives, pp. 1-2. Ransom to Bishop C.C. Alleyne, January 7, 1949, Ransom Papers, Wilberforce Univerisity Archives. Alleyne, an A.M.E.Z. Bishop and Ransom, a Bishop of the A.M.E. Church, discussed their concerns during the 1948 biennial meeting of the Federal Council of Churches held in Cincinnati, Ohio (1948).

[78]For another view of the unsuccessful attempts at church union from 1884 to 1972, see W.J. Walls, History of the African Methodist Episcopal Zion Church (Charlotte, North Carolina: A.M.E.Z. Publishing House, 1974), pp. 468-77.

[79]Walls, History of the A.M.E.Z. Church, pp. 490-91.

[80]Ransom, Memo re: Reorganization of the Fraternal Council of Negro Churches, p. 2; Ransom Papers, Wilberforce University Archives.

[81]John J. Carey, "The Intellectual World of Carlyle Marney." The Bulletin, Vol. 4, No. 1 (March 1980), p. 6.

CHAPTER IV

Social Gospel Influences

> Joseph Mazzini, the great Italian
> patriot, taught his fellow
> countrymen that the way to secure
> their liberation was through the
> fulfillment of their duties...He
> taught that it was not simply a
> man's right to be free, but that
> it was his duty, because God had
> created him to enjoy freedom, and
> therefore, he would make himself
> an instrument of thwarting the
> ends of his Creator if he
> permitted, without resistance,
> his freedom to be taken away.[1]

Ransom began his ministry at the beginning of the Progressive Era. The group of reformers that have been labelled progressives consisted of a wide assortment of people. Historian Carl Resak has characterized the Progressives in the following manner:

> This wide variety of individuals and groups held in common an attitude usually called "progressive." Though they might agree on little else, progressives shared the view that the social order could and must be improved and that such change must not await God's will, natural laws, including the laws of the market place, or any beneficient force.[2]

Thus, as Resak has pointed out, the Progressives were reformers, not revolutionaries. Specifically, they accepted, without question, the viability of the democratic system. The Progressives' intention was not to replace the internal structure of American society with another (i.e., Communist, etc.), but rather to reform existing labor and social structures. The feature that characterized Progressives was their belief that social, political and economic reforms could be achieved through social change.

The Progressives' major contention was that industrialized society had prohibited the individual's pursuit of happiness. They theorized that racial, economic and environmental factors prevented men from expressing their fullest human potential, and Progressives strove to correct that imbalance.

The Social Gospel Movement was the religious expression of the Progressive Era. Although essentially rural in its ethic, Protestantism's most significant attmept to reshape urban America was the Social Gospel Movement. Certainly, Protestant Christianity did not escape the ferment and controversy of the Progressive Era and the Protestant Church attempted to respond to the challenges and demands of an industrial and urban society. There were three concrete challenges that the Protestant Church defined as social and labor concerns: (1) labor and industrial problems, i.e., working hours, conditions, wages, etc.; (2) the exploitation of immigrant workers; and (3) the social maladjustments of rapid urbanization and industrialization, i.e., squalid housing, disease, juvenile delinquency, and rising crime. Progressives viewed such conditions as potentially destructive to society if such maladjustments were left unattended. The attempt of Social Gospelers to ameliorate urban difficulties was exacerbated by the economic uncertainty engendered by periodic depressions between 1873-77, 1883-86, and 1893-97.

However, not all Protestant clergymen agreed with their Social Gospel counterparts; for example, conservative clergymen did not recognize the seriousness of these ecnomic problems. Thus, they thought that periodic economic dislocations did not warrant a reordering of the social and economic system. They firmly believed that such wrongs would right themselves through a natural evolutionary process, and in this progression, only the fittest would survive.

Although the origins of the Social Gospel can be traced to the protestant evangelical movement of the 1840's and 1850's, its foundation was actually laid in the 1870's and 1880's with Social Gospelers reaching the peak of their activities in the late nineteenth and early twentieth centuries. Those same years (1890-1912) were pivotal ones in the developing thought and ministry of Reverdy C. Ransom, when, between 1890 and 1912, Ransom pastored large A.M.E. churches in Cleveland, Ohio, Chicago, Illinois, and New York City.

Since Social Gospelers believed that it was incumbent upon the church to alter the conditions which prevented an individual's growth, they contented that individual change was contingent upon societal change. This belief coincided with the sensibility that Ransom had received from the black church. In light of the racist mores and conditions of the nineteenth century, a major concern of the black church was to remove the stigma of inferiority from black consciousness. Thus, the mission of the church was to impart the concept that individual worth was not ultimately promulgated by white society, but rather, given by God. The underlying premise for this belief was that God had not created Blacks as inferior beings to the rest of His creation. [4] Wilberforce University affirmed these theological constructs through its teaching. As a graduate of Wilberforce, Ransom had been exposed to the evangelical belief in racial equality and individual perfection, and the Christian transformation of society.

Ransom's developing concept of ministry was nourished by two persons closely associated with Wilberforce University--Benjamin W. Arnett and Daniel A. Payne. Benjamin Arnett, who was Ransom's supporter and friend, served as trustee of one major organization that was related to the Social Gospel Movement--the United Society of Christian Endeavor.[5]

Christian Endeavor societies were composed of young men and women imbued with the idea of Christian charity and commitment. Christian Endeavor, founded by a Portland, Maine congregational minister, the Reverend Francis E. Clark, stressed that the inward call of faith was validated by its outward expression of service to the community. Through Christian Endeavor and many other Christian youth organizations that followed its pattern, thousands of idealistic young people enlisted and served as Social Christianity's missionaries to the urban centers of America.[6]

Arnett exposed Ransom to Christian Endeavor and other organizations, and often used his influence to provide Ransom with the opportunity to participate in them. In 1897, while pastoring Bethel A.M.E. Church in Chicago, Ransom accompanied Arnett to the International Convention of the United Society of Christian Endeavor held in San Francisco.[7] Such exposure allowed Ransom the opportunity to witness examples of Social Gospel structures which he would later institute in his own pastoral ministry.

In addition, Daniel Payne had introduced Ransom to the influential and fiercely liberal church paper, The Independent of New York. Payne stated to Ransom that "You cannot read it regularly without becoming an intelligent man."[8] The Independent represented the anti-slavery sentiment among American churches before the Civil War. The paper continued its support of black rights during Civil War-Reconstruction and long after other radical journals, such as The Nation and Harper's Weekly had ceased to support black rights. In subsequent years, The Independent became a leading exponent of Social Gospel.

An editor of The Independent (1871-75) and a leading Social Gospeler of the time was Washington Gladden. Historians Henry F. May and Aaron I. Abell have referred to Gladden as "the most influential of the Social Gospel's teachers and leaders."[9] This

75

observation is supported by the fact that Gladden was extremely active within the Social Gospel Movement and was author of Working People and Their Employers. This publication was considered "one of the mile-posts set by American Social Christianity."[10] Futhermore, this book set the Social Gospel Movement's positive approach and attitude toward the rights of labor. Gladden urged the church to become actively involved in an equitable solution to the crisis between working people and their employers. The application of "Christian Law," in his view, would necessitate fair play and simple justice for the worker.[11] Ransom's support of the working man, like Gladden's, was life-long. However, Ransom emphasized, as Gladden did not, the problem of racism and job discrimination within the American labor movement. Thus, it is important to recognize that Ransom began his ministry within a distinctive religious social and historical milieu. Outstanding Social Gospelers were vocalizing their tenets which had far-reaching effects in the development of the movement itself.

One such Social Gospel leader was Josiah Strong, who came into prominence in 1885 with the publication of his book, Our Country. He was a founder and officer of numerous Social Gospel organizations which included the Evangelical Alliance, the Open and Institutional Church League, the American Institute of Christian Sociology, the League for Social Science, and the American Institute for Social Science. Strong believed that the duty of the church was to serve the "entire man (in his) entire life." Strong thought that a clear grasp of Jesus' mission to the world would energize the church to "apply his salvation to body as well as soul, and to society as well as the individual."[12] Stong was recognized for his organizational skill and acumen, and he coordinated, in 1887, 1889 and 1893, the "three most significant" Social Gospel meetings held in the United States. The latter meeting, held in connection with the Chicago World's Fair and Exposition, was the World Parliament of Religions. Both meetings had a far-reaching impact on Ransom's life and his expanding thought and ministry. By attending the World's Fair and the Parliament of Religions, Ransom not only heard major Social Gospel theorists, including Washington Gladden, but he met others with whom he would soon be involved.

While perceiving the Columbian Expostion as the herald of a new age and century, Ransom considered the broadly ecumenical Parliament of Religions to have been the "crowding" achievement of the nineteenth century. In it, Ransom saw "Jesus binding together every nation and every people in faith, in brotherhood and in love."[13]

The Parliament emphasized the social mission of the church and the methods of accomplishing that task. The most popular of the conference's four program divisions was the category devoted to the church and social problems. Twelve major addresses considered the function of the church in a changing social order. Attendees in other sessions were informed about "the various aspects of religious social work such as the institutional church, athletics, tenement reform, politics, boys' clubs, and social settlements.[14] These and other concrete manifestations of the Social Gospel in action became central components in Ransom's working concept of the church, particularly during his pastorates in Chicago and New York. R.R. Wright, Jr., one of Ransom's contemporaries, suggested that it was in Chicago that Ransom "fell under the influence of the 'Social Gospel',"[15] and three of its most important advocates: Jane Addams and the Reverends Graham Taylor and Frank Gunsaulus.

Jane Addams was one of the most well-known Progressives of her times. She was the founder of Hull House which became an inspiration to the social settlement movement in the United States because it attempted to respond to the needs of Chicago's European immigrants. She was considered one of the greatest pioneers of charitable reform of her time. Ransom considered Addams to be one of the "finest personalities" he had ever known, and he called on her for advice and assistance during the formative period of the Institutional Church and Social Settlement which he founded in Chicago in 1900. It was due in part to Addams' influence that Ransom received significant financial support for the Institutional Church and Social Settlement from Chicago's white elite leaders such as Mrs. George Pullman and Mr. Robert L. Lincoln. Mrs. Pullman was the widow of the founder of the Pullman Railroad Company, and Robert L. Lincoln, son of President Lincoln, was president of the Pullman Company at that time. Both Robert Lincoln and Mrs. Pullman paid the salaries of three employees of the kindergarten school at the Institutional Church.[16]

Jane Addams' relationship with Ransom is

significant because she is one of the key persons, along with Graham Taylor, who indirectly provided Ransom with a format and structure that was useful in his Institutional Church. Graham Taylor was a blend of Social Gospel theory and practice. He was both academician and pastor. In 1880, Taylor became the pastor of the Fourth Congregational Church of Hartford, Connecticut. He organized that church to respond to the needs of its wage-earning residents. Through its outreach ministry, the church made its presence felt in the community by visiting and aiding families in distress. It supplied them with food, clothing, financial assistance, and other resources and opened its ministry to the indigent members of the community.

While pastoring Fourth Congregational, Taylor held seminars for pastors and theological students in which he explained the method and approach of his outreach program. By 1888, Hartford Theological Seminary had appointed him Professor of Practical Theology, providing him the platform to expand his developing theories of social Christianity. As a classroom teacher, Taylor stressed many of the central themes of the Social Gospel Movement: preaching, evangelism, pastoral care, economics and sociology.[17]

By 1893 and the World Parliament of Religions meeting, Graham Taylor had become a leading Social Gospel spokesman. The following year, he accepted the call of the Chicago Theological Seminary to assume its first chair of "Christian Sociology." He established the Chicago Commons Settlement as the laboratory for his classes and soon after accepted the pastorate of a struggling neighborhood congregation which he later housed within the settlement.[18] Reverdy C. Ransom, who arrived in Chicago to assume the pastorate of Bethel A.M.E. Church in 1896, had at his disposal models of ministry (Addams and Taylor) to which he could relate. There was Hull House on the westside and Chicago Commons on the southside. However, neither settlement was directly geared to the concerns of that city's expanding black community. Ransom remembered the "active sympathy and cooperation" of Jane Addams and Graham Taylor in the establishment and on-going activities of the Institutional Church and Social Settlement, and he sought to combine the best secular and social emphasis of social Christianity in that institution.[19]

While Ransom received help from Addams and Taylor

during his years in Chicago, he relied even more heavily
upon the frienship and intellectual companionship of
Frank Gunsaulus and Clarence Darrow. Both Gunsaulus and
Darrow were native Ohioans and shared many similar
interests. Gunsaulus and Ransom were outstanding
preachers and orators at the time when pulpiteers were
in vogue. Both ministers were popular lecturers. They
travelled nationwide to speak to various groups and
shared a tolerance and respect for all kinds of people.
These two men also shared political perspectives and
appealed for the freedom of Cuba in 1895, and for the
fair treatment of Puerto Rico and the Philippines in
1900.[20]

Arriving in Chicago in 1887, Gunsaulus had
expressed a key element of the Social Gosepel credo as
early as 1881. It was his conviction, then as well as
later, that theology must be translated into sociology.
By the time the World Parliament of Religions convened
in Chicago in 1893, Gunsaulus was a well-known Social
Gospeler, having joined the Chautaqua movement as a
lecturer on social Christianity in 1889.[21] Gunsaulus
was scheduled to address the Parliament on the subject
of "Protestantism in Eloquence and Literature," but was
unable to do so because of illness.[22] While pastoring
in Chicago Gunsaulus attracted the attention of
millionaire, Phillip D. Armour who founded the Armour
Meat Packaging Company. Armour was influenced by
Gunsaulus' sermons which addressed the problems of youth
unemployment in Chicago. Thus, Armour donated to
Gunsaulus two million dollars for construction of the
Armour Institute of Technology.[23] Orginally, the
Institute was established to provide technical training
to young urban dwellers. However, Gunsaulus was able to
combine and harmonize the technical training with moral
and intellectual training. It is significant to note
that the Institutional Church and Social Settlement
included a technical department for youth.[24]

A second Ohio compatriot of Ransom's was the
controversial and inconoclastic lawyer, Clarence Darrow
who was not a traditional religionist. His professional
career was marked by the championing of unpopular
causes. Characterized by his agnostic and inconoclastic
nature, Darrow was critical of the church's
provincialism, superstition and narrowness, and defended
the Socialist leader, Eugene V. Debs in the 1890's; "Big
Bill" hayward, the radical labor organizer (Industrial
Workers of the World) in the early 1900's; John T.

Scopes in the famous "Monkey" trial in Tennessee; Leopold and Loeb in the infamous murder trial in Chicago, and Dr. O.H. Sweet in the "Sweet Case" in Detroit during the 1920's. Darrow used his brilliant mind and sharply honed legal skills to defend the rights of those individuals and groups considered dangerous and unmanageable by the larger society.[25]

Darrow's friendly relationship with Ransom was based upon clear cut ideals and concepts that Darrow espoused on the issue of race. Darrow, an agnostic humanist, was also a well-known friend and supporter of Afro-American causes. He began his law practice in Chicago in the 1890's, and his clientele included a large number of Blacks at a time when few white lawyers would take their cases. A long-time members of the NAACP, he frequently offered legal expertise to the organization, gave time, talent and financial resources to many institutions, including clubs, lodges, and colleges. He lectured at Howard University Law School, wrote numerous articles for the black press, and frequently spoke at Bethel A.M.E. Church and the Institutional Church Social Settlement in Chicago during the years Reverdy Ransom pastored those institutions.[26]

Darrow believed racial hatred was the most incendiary form of intolerance and fought against it all his life. He was free of prejudice of any kind. Speaking about the matter of race, Darrow said, "When it comes to human beings, I am color blind. To me, people are not simply white or black, they are all freckled."[27] W.E.B. DuBois, constantly wary of and sensitive to the blatant and subtle prejudices of Whites, said about him, "I was drawn to Clarence Darrow because he was so absolutely lacking in racial consciousness and because of the broad catholicity of his knowledge and tastes."[28] It is clear why Ransom found Darrow such a sympathetic and warm friend during his Chicago ministry, since Ransom judged people, particularly Whites, on their freedom from prejudice. Thus, if they were able to meet Blacks as equals, Ransom was not concerned about their denominational or religious proclivity. As a proponent of racial and social equality, Darrow became a major contributor to Ransom's Social Gospel perspective. Ransom's expanding social theory was also influenced by a European, Guisseppi Mazzini. He is not unique in that experience, however. Winthrop S. Hudson, in Religion in America, indicates that "the developing social concern among American Protestants was stimulated in part by influences from abroad.[29] Scotland, England, Germany and Switzerland were centers of religious ferment on the Continent.[30]

A focal point for many of the Social Gospel leaders were the writings of Guisseppi Mazzini, referred to by many as the Abraham Lincoln of Italy. Mazzini was the source of inspiration for many of the theories which later emanated from and characterized the Social Gospel Movement. For example, it was Mazzini who first criticized the church for remaining reticent in areas of social conern. Secondly, he challendged the orthodoxy of the church and voiced the opinion that the church ought to lead in changing the society and correcting its social ills. The underlying premise was the belief that one must change the society _first_ and then the individual could be changed. Thirdly, it was from Mazzini's writings that Social Gospelers found support for their belief in God as the source of human equality. Finally, as a supporter of the rights of working men, Mazzini made one of his primary commitments to the workers. It was upon the shoulder of the working man that Mazzini believed democracy could be built.[31]

American Social Gopelers interpreted Mazzini's writing as criticism of the church as they understood it. One direct manifestation of the Social Gospeler's relationship to Mazzini was the organization referred to as the Brotherhood of the Kingdom. Mazzini's life and work exerted enormous influence on this important Social Gospel society. Originating in a friendship among three young Baptist ministers in New York during the late 1880's, the Brotherhood of the Kingdom was formed officially in 1892. One of the founders, Walter Rauschenbusch, later became the Social Gospel's most renowned theoretican. The Brotherhood, rarely exceeding 35 in number, met each summer from 1893 to 1915 to prayerfully consider and contemplate the Kingdom ideal as Jesus taught and practiced it and the Kingdom's relationship and applicability to their times. Some of the topics analyzed in their summer meetings included socialism the question of labor, monopolies, the ethics of business, and economic justice issues. From the discussions and deliberation of the confabs emerged many of the major themes of the Social Gospel Movement. The Brotherhood sought to reestablish the Kingdom of God idea in the thought of the church and to assist the church in realizing that concept in the world. Their gatherings were pervaded with a deeply religious sense

81

of purpose and mission to humanity. It was through prayer and serious reflection from the Bible, contemporary sociological and theological studies, and the writings of important religious thinkers that the directions for their ministries were revealed. For the strengthening of its meditational life, the Brotherhood frequently turned to the words and inspiration of Mazzzini.[32]

The Brotherhood was not alone in its high regard of Mazzini. The Episcopal Christian Social Union was another organization, similarly impressed. Founded in 1891 to educate the church regarding its ethical obligations to society, the Union devoted itself to the dissemination of information through conferences, lectures and the publication of numerous articles and pamphlets. Its montly, <u>Publications</u>, distributed through the country, dealt with many Social Gospel subjects, one of which was <u>Rights and Duties - Passages from the Writings of Joseph Mazzini</u>.[33] Key themes expressive of Mazzini's thought were absorbed and echoed by his disciples within the American Social Gospel Movement.

Mazzini was as important a figure and role model for Ransom as he had been to Ransom's white Social Gospel counterparts. There are three distinct occasions in which Ransom refers to Mazzini and his writings. On each of these occasions, Mazzini's thought became the argumentative basis upon which Ransom supported his own theories. Three of the articles appeard in the <u>A.M.E. Review</u> between 1896 and 1912. They were entitled "The Negro and Socialism," "A Programme for the Negro," and "Duty and Destiny."

Historian, Timothy L. Smith has observed that the uniqueness of the nineteenth century black religious consciousness was its adherence to the early Christian view of man's duty and destiny.[34] Ransom believed that God did not create Blacks to acquiese in the face of injustice, but rather he thought that man himself was responsible for injustices. Therfore, since man creates the conditions of injustice, then he must bear the responsibility (as a duty) of changing those conditions. In Ransom's view, black people were destined to live in world without racial or social injustice. In a 1904 Thanksgiving address, entitled "Duty and Destiny," delivered at Bethel A.M.E. Church in New Bedford, Massachusetts and published in part in the April 1905

A.M.E. Review, Ransom posed the question of personal and collective destiny. Questioning whether one' destiny was "a part of a fixed order in the scheme of things or something to be attained (or) achieved...by capacity, courage (and) and character," Ransom based his answer on the teachings of Jesus. Paraphrasing Mazzini, Ransom wrote that in dealing with the great question of human rights, Jesus never taught men how to obtain their rights, but always taught them how to fulfill their duties...to God and their fellow's man.[35] Ransom thought that it was black people's God-given duty to use whatever means necessary to maintain their freedom. This concept is clearly delineated by Ransom in a 1913 editorial which took its title from one of Mazzini's essays, "Rights and Duties." In that editorial, Ransom indicated that Blacks were duty-bound to maintain their freedom, and to relinquish this duty would demean and deny God from whom this freedom came.

Mazzini's challenge to the workingmen of Italy is echoed by Ransom when he advances the proposition that all men have a right to work and support their households. It was their duty to demand shorter work hours in order to have the leisure time so necessary for family and friends. As far as wages were concerned, man was duty bound to make demands for a just share of the fruit of his labor. Similarly, Ransom believed that it was the black man's duty to demand employment and protect his home from assault.

Education, according to Ransom, was also a right, and black people were duty-bound to "fight any limitation, curtailment or discrimination" which would deny them equal educational opportunities and advancement. In this editorial, Ransom challenged his readers to understand the fact that with the right to vote came the duty to vote. If that right was "denied, abridged or menaced," it was the duty of Blacks to fight their exclusion from the political process with every means at their disposal.[36] Thus, Mazzini's beliefs and the ideas emanating from the religious ferment of the times influenced Ransom's Social Gospel thought and actions. Similar to most Social Gospelers, Ransom was influenced by the developing science of sociology. Social Science became allied with Social Christianity. It became science in the service of religion.[37]

Thus, Social Gospelers, with their fellow Progressives, believed in the power and efficacy of data and research. Once truth was objectively presented and analyzed, the wheels of reform would be set in motion. The need for such knowledge was apparant as the church set out to devise an approach to urban society. Recognizing the need to develop data to assist the church and its ministry in reform activities, a number of seminaries in the 1880's and 1890's established sociology courses within their curricula.[38] One Social Gospel agency among many founded in 1898 to collect and disseminate data for reform purposes was the "League for Social Science," later called the American Institute for Social Science.[39] Furthermore, many of the new social science techniques were presented at national and local chuch conferences and gatherings, and sociology and reform became key allies of the Social Gospel Movement.

The religious census and the community survey were just two of the approaches used by Social Gospelers to ascertain the needs of a neighborhood and plan a church program to meet them. Such social science techniques resulted in the establishment of institutional churches and religious social settlements. One Social Gospeler called it "Practical Sociology in the Service of Social Ethics" while the adage "Christianity Practically Applied" became not only an indentifying phrase of the movement, but also became the name of a Social Gospel journal devoted to the reform of society.[40]

Ransom was closely associated with four Blacks trained in sociological research: Richard R. Wright, Monroe N. Work, George E. Haynes and W.E.B. DuBois. Wright and Work were young ministerial assistants to Ransom during his pastorate at Chicago's Institutional Church and Social Settlement (1900-1904). Both men gained valuable experiential knowledge of urban life from such interchanges. Wright was a research fellow in sociology at the University of Pennsylvania from 1906 to 1908. Wright received his Ph.D. degree in sociology from that university in 1911, becoming the first Black in the United States to achieve that distinction. His doctoral dissertation, "The Negro in Pennsylvania, A Study of Economic History," was published in 1912. Monroe N. Work, head of Tuskegee's Department of Research and Records, edited the data-filled volumes of the Negro Yearbook for many years. George E. Haynes who worked with Ransom during the latter's editorship of the A.M.E. Review, studied sociology at Yale, the New York School of Philanthropy, and Columbia University.[41] He was the first chairman of Fisk University's Social Science Department and a founder of the National League on Urban Conditions Among Negroes (later named the National Urban League).

Despite the excellent contributions of Ransom's younger colleagues, his fellow militant, W.E.B. DuBois, with whom he participated in the Afro-American Council, the Niagara Movement and the NAACP, was the unquestioned elder statesman of black sociology. His studies of black life beginning in the late 1890's under the sponsorship of Atlanta University were a part of the progressive thrust for research and data. Articulating with his usual sharpness the ethos of the time, DuBois wrote, "The Negro problem was in my mind a matter of systematic investigation and intelligent understanding. The world was wrong about race, because it did not know. The ultimate evil was stupidity. The cure for it was knowledge based on scientific information."42 Called to Philadelphia in 1896 by the University of Pennsylvania to do a study of the city's seventh ward, DuBois saw the study as "an opportunity...to put science into sociology through a condition and problem of my own group."43 The study, which became his classic work, The Philadelphia Negro, was intended to present to the powers in Philadelphia exactly what the black Philadelphian's problems were in order that a solution to those problems might be effected. His task was to disseminate the truth. However, the findings were ignored.

Ransom, unlike DuBois, did not have the scholar's commitment to systematic intellectual inquiry. However, he was convinced that research and data about the church could be used to inspire black people to continue the struggle for racial advancement and impress that determination upon white people. The black church, in Ransom's mind, was the highest cultural achievement within the race's religious and secular life. Ransom's interest in social research manifested itself first in his editorship of the A.M.E. Yearbooks and later in his editing of the Yearbook of Negro Churches, which were an attempt by Negro churches "to recognize fully and without bias the endeavors of all denominations..."44 His involvement with The Yearbooks continued through the 1940's. The studies gave statistical data on black church membership; finances; church property; educational endeavors; Sunday Schools; ministers' salaries; and domestic and foreign missions. These statistical emphases were an indication of Ransom's interest and commitment to research and its dissemination of factual information in the service of the church and society.

Another practical expression of Ransom's willingness to use all available means to espouse the cause of racial and social justice is most clearly revealed in his editorship of the <u>A.M.E. Review</u>. Like so many of his Social Gospel colleagues, he was a believer in the power of the press in effecting social change. According to Robert T. Handy, Social Gospelers "...in the years prior to World War I...were highly articulate in pulpit, platform and press and evoked wide interest in social questions."[45] As powerful preacher, magnificent orator, and fighting editor, Ransom fits Handy's description perfectly.

In a speech delivered before the General Conference of the A.M.E. Church soon after his election as editor of the Review, Ransom said,

> The printed page has superseded the spoken word as a means for dissemination of know-ledge. The carrying power of the human voice has but a narrow range. The preacher, lecturer or orator may at best address but a few thousand souls, but when the press takes up his word, he may speak to an audience as vast as the circumference of the globe. The present opportunities of Negro journalism, religious or otherwise, hold potentialties of incalculable influence an power.[46]

The A.M.E. Church, the forerunner among black denominations, had developed its publication appraratus almost immediately after its establishment in 1816 in order to instruct and educate its members, not only about church doctrice and discipline, but about living and functioning in the world. Black clergymen, leaders in the broader community, as well as in the church, used the press to address their secular and sacred constituents about the critical issues of the day.[47] That was an aspect of the milieu in which Ransom moved as a seminarian and young pastor.

In 1817, a year after its founding, the church organized a Department of Publication, pioneering and taking the lead among later black denominations in the field. Incorporated under the laws of Pennsylvania in 1855, it became the A.M.E. Book Concern. An A.M.E.

layman, Samuel E. Cornish, along with John B. Russwurm, started the first black newspaper, Freedom's Journal in 1827. It and other black newspapers of the period were short-lived. However, in 1848, the A.M.E. Bishops started the Christian Herald newspaper and changed its name to the Christian Recorder in 1852. In 1884, the A.M.E. Church Quarterly Review was begun by Benjamin T. Tanner who was elected to the episcopacy four years later. Ransom was exposed to the Christian Recorder in his childhood and youth, and was well aware of both the Recorder and Review during the 1880's while studying at Wilberforce and pastoring churches in Ohio and Pennsylvania.

Ransom's enthusiasm and interest in statistics and journalism were undoubtedly generated prior to his Social Gospel involvement. His friend and mentor, Benjamin W. Arnett, was statistician, financial secretary, and editor of the Budget of the A.M.E. Church for many years.[48] As a researcher, Ransom assisted Arnett in the preparation of the Budget. Furthermore, the A.M.E. Church, coming out of the Wesleyan tradition of church polity and episcopacy, was historically methodical and precise in keeping records. At the conclusion of any A.M.E. Annual Conference report can be found statistical tables covering many aspects of the church; conversions, full members, persons on probation, church societies and auxiliaries, churches and their seating capacities, baptisms, marriages, deaths, pastor's salary, value of church property, along with a complete Statistical Table relating to every facet of the Sunday School.

The prestige, influence and power associated with the editorial leadership of the A.M.E. newspapers and journals was considerable. They provided an editor with a national platform from which to speak and to become known within the church.

During the 1880's, Ransom was a correspondent from his annual conference to the A.M.E. Christian Recorder and a regular contributor in the 1890's to the Indianapolis Freeman. A frequent essayist, Ransom's articles and lectures were published in numerous magazines and journals. In fact, the decades of the 1880's was a period of tremendous growth for many black newspapers. In 1870, there were ten black newspapers in the United States. By 1880, the number had increased to thirty-one, and by 1890, had increased again about five

87

times, numbering 154.[49]   Two additional A.M.E.
newspapers began in the decade - the Southern Christian
Recorder in 1886 and the Western Christian Recorder in
1891. Both journals were indicative of the growth of
the A.M.E. Church in those geographical areas between
1865 and 1890.[50]   Although there was a rather high
mortality rate among the secular newspapers, the fact of
their existence indicated racial progress. The race was
establishing its own institutions, none more crucial in
Ransom's view than the press, for through it, messages
of hope, direction and inspiration could be communicated
to the great mass of black people, both the churched and
the unchurched.

    Ransom's interest in the press began prior to his
association with the A.M.E. Review. It actually began
during his pastorate in Allegheny City, Pennsylvania
when he became associate editor of a newspaper that was
called the Afro-American Spokesman. According to
Ransom, literally hundreds of Blacks lived in "wretched
tenements in the alleys and on shanty boats along the
waterfront,"[51] where the church was located. Through
intimate association with a group of leading ministers,
Ransom, the youngest cleric among them, joined them in
establishing a newspaper that was designed to encourage
black solidarity in action against social ills.

    By 1900, having gained notice within church circles
as a dynamic preacher, skillful church administrator,
and able journalist, Ransom was touted for the
editorship of the Christian Recorder, since its editor
at the time was seeking election to the Bishopric. The
editor's attempt was unsuccessful and he was re-elected
for another four-year term. Ransom was elected to the
position of editor of the A.M.E. Church Review during
the A.M.E. General Conference held in St. Louis in 1912.

    Ransom saw a mission and purpose in the A.M.E.
Church Review. He insisted that it was created and
should be maintained "as a literary forum where
Americans of African descent could state and plead their
cause at the bar of public opinion."[52]   During his
editorship, according to Ransom, there were few journals
which gave black people the opportunity to express
"their side of controversial questions relating to the
race."[53]   Ransom wrote that the purpose of the Review
was "to inform, to stimulate, enlighten and possibly
inspire and strengthen the high purpose of a class of
people who are leaders in their sphere of action (and

88

that) is indeed a most engaging task."[54] During his
twelve-year tenure as editor, Ransom directed the Review
down interrelated paths. Convinced that the journal
provided Blacks with an unprecednented literary forum,
he stated four immediate objectives: (1) under his
editorial leadership, its contributors would represent
the highest and best in "Negro scholarship" and thought
in the United States and abroad;[55] (2) the journal would
be a major vehicle in the effort to provide continuing
education for the church and its ministry; (3) it would
cover and report any and all major development "in
theology, ethics, the church, religion, science,
philosophy, politics, sociology, literature and
art,"[56] and (4) it would be a journal of protest and
agitation for black rights. Under Ransom's leadership,
the Review continued to address the issues of the day
and also broadened its ecumenical base. The subcription
list numbered approximately twenty-six hundred and thus
Ransom was well assured that the journal was guiding and
shaping public opinion. The topics it covered were
numerous and included law, medicine, ministry, education
and social welfare. In essence, his audience was the
black educated and elite, or, as DuBois had called them,
"the talented tenth."

In a report on the Review that he presented to the
Twenty-Seventh General Conference (1924), Ransom stated
that the Review's uniqueness could be found in its
religious sensibility--"a sensibility predisposing it to
view all great questions without passion or prejudice in
the light of the Cross of Christ."[57] However, one might
doubt whether under Ransom's tutelage the Review was
"without passion or prejudice," there is little doubt
but that the pages reflect his determined effort to
shape its spirit and essence in accordance with his
racial and social vision.

In 1918, believing strongly in a cooperative effort
and maintaining a relationship with other leading
publications, Ransom arranged to offer his readers both
the Review and the Crisis at a subcription rate of $1.50
for a year. Ransom felt that such an offering provided
black leaders with the most informative analysis of
racial life from secular and religious perspectives. In
short, both the Crisis and the Review were vehicles for
maintaining and defending the integrity of the black
race.[58] Ransom recruited persons who would assist him
in the development of the Review. From a critical and
evaluative standpoint, the Review can be used as a gauge

to measure Ransom's philosophical predilections. As an editor, Ransom solicited works from knowledgeable and competent people who could denomstrate a commitment to the race and its advancement. Two regular contributors, as well as associate editors, included Dr. George E. Haynes and George Forbes.

By 1909, Haynes was a student at the New York School of Philanthropy (now known as the New School for Social Science Research). It was here that he became interested in problems which arose from the increased migration of Blacks into New York City. The concern that Haynes had for the economic difficulties experienced by the migrating black population became the dissertation topic he submitted to Columbia Universtiy. In 1912, he was the first black man to receive the Ph.D. from Columbia University, and his dissertation, "The Negro at Work in New York City," was published as a book and was primarily a sociological study. Haynes' professional and academic activities and associations placed him, in many respects, within the Social Gospel Movement.[59] Like Ransom, Haynes believed that religion had to be relevant and thus practically applicable to the current condition of the world. On this and many other issues, Ransom and Haynes shared similar viewpoints. Neither Ransom nor Haynes was content with the traditional religious practices of their numerous associates, and therefore, they were opposed to the (traditonal) contemporary emphasis of the church on prayer meetings and Bible readings. Both men viewed such activities as insufficient means to address current issues. Thus, it is not surprising that immediately following his election to editorship of the A.M.E. Review, Ransom asked Haynes to join his staff as associate editor in the department of "Social Science." The department was merely the rubric under which Haynes contributed a series of social science articles. Furthermore, as editor of the Review, Ransom was forthright in stating the overall tone and direction that the magazine would take when he stated the following:

> ...We shall concern ourselves, not less about Israel in Egypt, but more about the Negro in America; not less about the Hebrews in the "fiery furnace," but more about Negroes burnt at the stake; not less about the daughters of Jerusalem by the rivers of Babylon, but more about

about our own daughters on the banks
of the Mississippi; not less about
Paul in the Phillipian jail or his
appeal to Caesar, but more about the
prison pens and peonage camps of the
South and our own appeal for political
and social justice in the United
States.[60]

In line with the current Progressivist theory of
emphasizing facts and truth, Ransom and Haynes were
confident that an enlightened public opinion would
support change. Being deeply committed Christians, both
men measured America's Christianity and democratic creed
by America's treatment of black people.

They were alike in their concerns about race and
both were basic believers in the power of Christianity
and the church to bring about racial and social change.
The purpose of the Department of Social Science was to
be "a medium of interpretation of the economic and
social forces and impulses of the growing social
consciousness of our times."[61] Its task was to keep the
readers of the _Review_ abreast of social and econmic
conditions within the world and describe how various
world movements for social change related to Christian
principles. According to Haynes, the Department had a
special obligation "to interpret the share the Negro has
in the world movement, as he is rising through his
growing race into the broader consciousness of humanity.
We shall try to bring our readers the ways in which the
Negro struggle, both in America and elsewhere, can be
common to the people of color."[62]

Haynes and Ransom shared the desire to illuminate
for black Americans the race's links with all black
freedom fighters. Addressing the 1912 A.M.E. General
Conference on the role the _A.M.E. Church Review_ should
play in the world-wide drama for justice, Ransom saw the
community of black struggle from the vantage point of
theology, and stated that

Our pulpit and our press have a distinct
mission a special message for the Negro
in particular, and generally for the
dark-skinned races of mankind, namely
this--that the Negro has a soul and that
Christ has not prepared him an inferior
hand of redemption...[63]

The Review attempted to bring to and reinforce for its readers the approbation that no nation could no long deny Blacks their human rights, since those rights came from God.

Haynes contributed two significant articles to Ransom's first issue. In the first article Haynes proposed that it was the responsibility of the church and the individual Christian to intelligently understand the forces at work in society if the two were to change the conditions under which people lived. Haynes' second article, "The Church and Social Science," appealed to the church to affirm its mission as God's instrument to implement the religious ideal of the Kingdom of God on earth. Haynes insisted that the questions facing the church were questions of man's relationship to man, and like Ransom, he hoped that the church could liberate itself to realize "the true Gospel to the settlement of race problems, to the betterment of living conditions in city and country, and to the abolition of every form of social injustice." [64] Voicing a concern which was not generally considered by white Social Gospelers, Haynes urged the church to address such racial issues by responding to the "treatment of darker and weaker races by lighter and stronger ones." [65]

Haynes remained on the staff of the Review for one year, and during that time specifically wrote on such appropriate topics as the "Social Betterment of Negroes in Cities," "The National Association for the Advancement of Colored People," and "The Negro and Organized Labor." [66]

The second individual who was asked by Ransom to become an associate editor was George W. Forbes, a native Mississipian, who received his education and training at Wilberforce University and Amherst College. Forbes received his M.A. degree in literature and arts from Amherst College in 1892, and then became editor of the Boston Courant. He remained at that position until 1897 when he was appointed reference libarian at the Boston Public Library. At that time, such a position was considered a prestigious one for a black person. He continued as libarian until his death more than thirty years later. In 1901, Forbes and Monroe Trotter established the militantly anti-Booker T. Washington newspaper, The Guardian. [67] In 1912, Ransom asked Forbes to join the staff of the Review as associate editor for the department, "In the Realm of Letters." Prior to offering Forbes this position, Ransom had been acquainted with him, both having been members of the Boston group led by Monroe Trotter which had expressed anti- (Booker T.) Washington sentiment in the early 1900's. Forbes remained with the Review until October 1918. During his tenure with the Review, Forbes reviewed books by numerous black authors, some of whom included James Welson Johnson, W.E.B. DuBois, Paul Lawrence Dunbar, Kelly Miller and Carter G. Woodson. Forbes also addressed subjects under the general topic of theatre arts and specifically wrote articles such as "The Colored Man and the Stage," discussed theatrical persons such as the black Shakespearian actor, Ira Aldridge and Bert Williams, a popular and well-known vaudeville commedian. Forbes' critiques covered topics like "Socialism under Marx and Engels" and the highly controversial film, "Birth of a Nation." Generally, Forbes' wide-ranging interests and articles encompassed geography, history, the West Indies, music, politics, and poetry.

Ransom assessed Forbes' contribution in the following manner when he wrote, "He has given to the Review a unique distinction, for nowhere else can be found a comprehensive survey of the whole domain of letters." [68] Thus, under the direction of Forbes, the department "In the Realm of Letters" became a forum in which the works of twentieth-century black writers were highlighted.

As a result of its broad-ranging base of interests, the Review distinguished itself in much the same way as did the Crisis. Both publications were the only (black) nationally recognized journals to support black authors whose racial pride and consciousness was a major focus for their craft. Therefore, it is clear that Ransom deliberately sought the best contributors available in his attempt to make the Review the epitome of black journalism. In writing to the novelist, Charles H. Chestnut, Ransom stated the following:

> ...What I am trying to do is to make the Review compel attention in this nation. To strike, I strike hard, to reach out initially in those directions which so seriously affect the larger interests of our people.

Consequently, he urged Chestnutt to become a frequent contributor to the Review, and asked him the question,

"Why should you not come out here with me and let us make this place a literary firing line, with the highest and best things?"[69]

Thus, under Ransom's leadership, some of America's most prestigious figures contributed to the Review, and in any issue from 1912 to 1924, one could fine essays by W.S. Scarborough, Kelly Miller and Charles W. Chestnutt; poems by Georgia Douglas Johnson, Fenton Johnson and James Weldon Johnson; or historical essays by John W. Cromwell, Arthur Schomburg and John Edward Bruce, as well as a broad variety of contributions by Daniel Hale Williams, William Monroe Trotter, Booker T. Washington, T. Thomas Fortune, Moorfield Storey, Oswald Garrison Villard and Ray Stannard Baker.[70]

Although these contributors held different opinions regarding the solution to the ractial problem, they shared a general concern for America's racial situation. Ransom's contribution to the racial issue was a series of editorials which covered lynching; disfranchisement; unemployment; unequal justice, and discriminatory education; the Jim Crow system; and the hypocrisy of white Christianity on racial matters. He challenged white America's conscience and urged continuing black resolve in the struggle for equal rights.

Ransom also wrote numerous editorials which dealt with the church and its ministry. Also, a large number of Review articles were intended to provide both the clergy and the laity with practical methodologies to better service their communities. Rarely was an issue published that did not contain at a minimum, one article on the subject of the church. Entire issues were devoted to such subjects as "Preparation for the Ministry," "The Minister in His Study," "The Minister as a Businessman for the Church," "The Minister in Relation to Church Entertainments and Social Diversion," "Sunday Manners for the Minister and Congregation," and many others.[71]

Thus, Ransom had set out intentionally to mold the Review in such a fashion that the broad issues facing the church, the race, American society and the world would be addressed. In large measure, he was successful in balancing those concerns. Ransom brought to the Review numerous literary contributions and articles concerning the church and its mission in the world, and most of these were consistent with his own activist vision of the church.

94

Footnotes

[1]Reverdy C. Ransom, "William Lloyd Garrison," The Centennial Oration, delivered in Fanueuil Hall, Boston, Massachusetts, December 11, 1905, The Spirit of Freedom and Justice (Nashville, 1926), pp. 9-10.

[2]Carl Resak, ed., The Progressives (New York: Bobbs-Merrill, 1967), p. xi.

[3]Aaron I. Abell, The Urban Impact on American Protestantism 1865-1900 (Cambridge: Harvard Unversity Press, 1943), pp. 3-26, 57-87; C. Howard Hopkins, The Rise of the Social Gospel in American Protestantism 1865-1915 (New Haven: Yale University Press, 1940), pp. 34-35; Robert T. Handy, A Christian America: Protestant Hopes and Historical Realities (New York: Oxford University Press, 1971), p. 156.

[4]Timothy L. Smith, "Slavery and Theology: The Emergence of Black Christian Consciousness in Nineteenth Century America," Church History, 41 (December, 1972), p. 504.

[5]Richard R. Wright, Jr., The Bishops of the African Methodist Episcopal Church (Nashville: The A.M.E. Sunday School Union, 1963).

[6]Abell, The Urban Impact on American Protestantism, pp. 210-14.

[7]B.W. Beckett, "Our Trip to the Christian Endeavor Convention," Christian Recorder (August 26, 1897), pp. 1,6; Ransom, Pilgrimage, p. 138.

[8]Ransom, "Editorial, William Hayes Ward," A.M.E. Review (October, 1916), p. 93.

[9]May, Protestant Churches and Industrial America, p. 171; Abell, The Urban Impact on American Protestantism, p. 70.

[10]Hopkins, The Rise of the Social Gospel, p. 27.

[11]Hopkins, The Rise of the Social Gospel, p. 29.

[12]Hopkins, The Rise of the Social Gospel, p. 115.

[13]Ransom, "Out of the Midnight Sky," A

Thanksgiving Address delivered at Mt. Zion

Congregational Church, Cleveland, Ohio, November 30, 1893, pp. 5-8, Ransom Papers, Wilberforce

University Archives.

[14]Hopkins, The Rise of the Social Gospel, pp. 115-16.

[15]Wright, Bishops of the A.M.E. Church, pp. 289-90.

[16]Ransom, Pilgrimage, pp. 88, 105, 112. The employees consisted of two teachers and the pianist of the kindergarten.

[17]Abell, The Urban Impact on American Protestantism, pp. 151-52, 234, 236-7. Books authored by Taylor include Religion in Social Action, with an introduction by Jane Addams (New York: Dodd & Mead Co., 1913), Pioneering on Social Frontiers (Chicago: University of Chicago Press, 1930) and Chicago Commons Through Forty Years (Chicago: Chicago Commons Association, 1936.

[18]Hopkins, The Rise of the Social Gospel, pp. 157, 167, 168; White & Hopkins, Religion and Reform in Changing America, pp. 139-59.

[19]Ransom, Pilgrimage, p. 104.

[20]"Doctor Gunsaulus: The Citizen, "An address given by the friends of Frank Wakely Gunsaulus, by Edgar C. Bancroft, April 24, 1921, pp. 4-7. Willard B. Gatewood, Black Americans and the White Man's Burden, 1893-1903 (Urbana: University of Illinois Press, 1975), pp. 253, 254; Ransom to Arthur Spingarn, December 31, 1930 refers to Gunsaulus as his "dear friend." Arthur B. Spingarn Paper, Moorland-Spingarn Research Center, Howard University.

[21]Bancroft, "Doctor Gunsaulus," pp. 1-2; Hopkins, Rise of the Social Gospel, p. 163.

[22]Hanson, The World's Congress of Religions, p. 1054.

[23]Newton, Some Living Masters of the Pulpit, pp.

248-49; Bancroft, "Doctor Gunsaulus," pp. 1-2.

[24] Ransom, _Pilgrimage_, pp. 81, 86, 113; Newton, Some _Living Masters of the Pulpit_, p. 246.

[25] Herbert Aptheker, ed., _The Correspondence of W.E.B. DuBois_, 1868-1963 (Amherst: University of Massachusetts Press, 1973), p. 190. On John T. Scopes and the "Monkey Trial," Leopold-Loeb and the Bobby Frank murder case, and Dr. O.H. Sweet and the Sweet trial, see Robert L. Allen, _Reluctanct Reforms: Racism and Social Reform Movements in the United States_ (New York: Anchor Books, 1975), pp. 201-5.

[26] Irving Stone, _Clarence Darrow for the Defense_ (New York: Doubleday & Co., 1941), pp. 96, 101, 170; Helen Buckler, _Doctor Dan_ (Boston: Little Brown & Co., 1954), p. 224.

[27] Stone, _Clarence Darrow for the Defense_, p. 70.

[28] Stone, _Clarence Darrow for the Defense_, p. 471.

[29] Winthrop S. Hudson, _Religion in America_, 2nd ed. (New York: Charles Scribner's Sons, 1973), p. 310.

[30] Hudson, _Religion in America_, p. 310.

[31] Essays: Selected from the writings, literary, political and religious, of Joseph Mazzini (London: W. Scott publisher, 1887); Henry Demarest Lloyd, _Mazzini and Other Essays_ (New York: G.P. Putnam & sons, 1910); Ignazio Silone, _The Living Thought of Mazzini_ (New York: Longmans, Green & Co., 1939); Joseph Mazzini, _The Duties of Man and Other Essays_ (New York: E.P. Dutton & Co., 1910). For a full and concise treatment of Mazzini's thought, see Ernest Rhys, ed., Essays: _The Duties of Man and Other Essays_ by Joseph Mazzini (New York: E.P. Dutton & Co., 1936), pp. 7-122.

[32] Hopkins, _The Rise of the Social Gospel_, pp. 131-33.

[33] Hopkins, _The Rise of the Social Gospel_, p. 166; Rosenberg, _Mazzini: The Prophet of the Religion of Humanity_, pp. 27, 26; Smith, "Slavery and Theology; the Emergence of Black Christian Consciousness in Nineteenth Century America," p. 504; Herbert Aptheker, ed., _A Documentary History of the Negro People in the United

States, Vol. 1 (new York: The Citadel Press, 1969), p. 283; Charles Spencer Smith, A History of the African Methodist Episcopal Church (Philadelphia: Book Concern of the A.M.E. Church, 1922), p. 42; George A. Singleton, The Romance of African Methodism (New York: Exposition Press, 1952), p. 43.

[34]Smith, "Slavery and Theology: The Emergence of Black Christian Consciousness in Nineteenth Century America," p. 497.

[35]Ransom, "Duty and Destiny," A.M.E. Review (April, 1905), pp. 316-17.

[36]Ransom, "Editorial, Rights and Duties," A.M.E. Review (July, 1913), pp. 52-56.

[37]Hopkins, The Rise of the Social Gospel, pp. 257-79.

[38]May, Protestant Churches and Industrial America, p. 194.

[39]Hopkins, The Rise of the Social Gospel, pp. 259-60.

[40]Hopkins, The Rise of the Social Gospel, pp. 257-78, 112; May, Protestant Churches and Industrial America, p. 194.

[41]Wright, 87 Years Behind the Black Curtain, p. 94; The Bishops of the A.M.E. Church, pp. 371-72; Samuel K. Roberts, "George Edmund Haynes: Advocate for Interracial Cooperation," in Randall K. Burkett and Richard Newman, eds., Black Apostles: Afro-American Clerty Confront the Twentieth Century (Boston: G.K. Hall & Co., 1978), p. 106; The Negro Handbook, compiled by the Editors of Ebony (Chicago: Johnson Publishing Co., Inc., Sociologists: Historical and Contemporary Perspectives (Chicago: University of Chicago Press, 1974), pp. 139-40, 238.

[42]W.E.B. DuBois, Dusk of Dawn: An Essay Toward and Autobiography of a Race Concept (New York: Schocken Books, 1968), p. 58.

[43]DuBois, Dusk of Dawn, p. 5.

[44]Ransom edited the A.M.E. Yearbook along with

C.S. Smith and John R. Hawkins, 1917-1918. See <u>A.M.E.</u> <u>Review</u> (June, 1918), pp. 190-91. Again in 1922-1923 Ransom, with the assistance of John R. Hawkins and Bishop John Hurst, edited the <u>A.M.E. Yearbook</u>. During the 1930's and early 1940's, Ransom broadened the <u>Yearbook</u> concept to include every major black denomination. Under his editorship, the <u>Yearbook of</u> <u>Negro Churches</u> was published by the A.M.E. Book Concern in 1935-1936 and 1939-1940. These and other volumes are located in the archives of Wilberforce University.

[45]Handy, <u>A Christian America</u>, p. 159.

[46]Ransom, "The Mission of the Religious Press," <u>The Spirit of Freedom and Justice</u>, p. 96.

[47]Woodson, <u>The History of the Negro Church</u>, pp. 149-50.

[48]Wright, <u>The Bishops of the A.M.E. Church</u>, p. 78.

[49]Detweiler, <u>The Negro Press in the United States</u>, p. 60.

[50]Bucke, <u>History of Methodism</u>, p. 548.

[51]Ransom, <u>Pilgrimage</u>, pp. 47-49. The Spokesman undoubtedly suffered an early death as did many of the black publications of the period. For a discussion of the early demise of such newspapers, see Detweiler, <u>The</u> <u>Negro Press in the United States</u>, p. 24.

[52]<u>Minutes of the Twenty-Seventh Quadrennial</u> <u>Session, A.M.E. General Conference</u>, Louisville, Kentucky, May, 1924, p. 384.

[53]Ransom, "Editorial, Agitation and Publicity," <u>A.M.E. Review</u> (January, 1920), p. 433.

[54]Ransom, "Editorial, The Editor's Chair," <u>A.M.E.</u> <u>Review</u> (April, 1920), pp. 507-08.

[55]Ransom, "Editorial, The Preacher-Editor," <u>A.M.E.</u> <u>Review</u> (July, 1912), p. 81.

[56]Ransom, <u>The Spirit of Freedom and Justice</u>, pp. 94, 97.

[57]<u>Minutes of the Twenty-Seventh Quadrennial</u>

Session of the A.M.E. General Conference, May, 1924, pp. 384-85.

[58]Ransom, "Editorial, The A.M.E. Church Review and the Crisis," A.M.E. Review (January, 1918), pp. 188-90.

[59]Samuel K. Roberts, "George Edmund Haynes: Advocate for Interracial Cooperation," in Burkett & Newman, ed., Black Apostles: Afro-American Clergy Confront the Twentieth Century, p. 98. Ransom, Pilgrimage, pp. 22-27.

[60]Ransom, "Editorial, The Preacher-Editor," A.M.E. Review (July 12, 1912), p. 81.

[61]Haynes, "The Department of Social Service," A.M.E. Review (July, 192), p. 72.

[62]Haynes, "The Department of Social Service," p. 72.

[63]Ransom, The Spirit of Freedom and Justice, p. 93.

[64]Haynes, "The Church and Social Service," A.M.E. Review (July, 1912), pp. 73-74.

[65]Haynes, "The Church and Social Service," p. 74.

[66]A.M.E. Review (October, 1912, July, 1913).

[67]Stephen R. Fox, The Guardian of Boston: William Monroe Trotter (New York: Atheneum, 1970), pp. 29-30.

[68]Ransom, "Editorial, George W. Forbes," p. 156.

[69]Ransom to Charles W. Chestnutt, July 28, 1913). Chestnutt Papers, Fisk University.

[70]Scarborough, a noted Greek scholar, author and long-time faculty member at Wilberforce University, was president of that institution from 1908 to 1920. Miller was professor and Dean at Howard Unviersity and considered a leading intellectual and academician of the day. Chestnutt was a leading author of the period, having written novels such as The Conjure Woman and

Other Tales, The Wife of His Youth and Other Stores of the Color Line, The House Behind the Cedars, The Marrow of Tradition and The Colonel's Dream. Ransom and Chestnutt knew each other first during Ransom's pastorate at Cleveland's St. John's A.M.E. Church from 1893 to 1896.

Georgia Douglas Johnson's work has been anthologized in James Welson Johnson's The Book of Negro Poetry (New York: Harcourt, Brace & World, 1959), pp. 181-84; The Negro Caravan, edited by Sterling Brown, Arthur P. David and Ulysses Lee (New York: The Citadel Press, 1941), pp. 339-40 and Arna Bontemps, ed., American Negro Poetry (New York: Hill and Wang, 1963), pp. 23-24. Fenton Johnson, considered by one literary critic as a participant in the making of America's new poetry, was born in Chicago in 1888. See Jean Wagner, Black Poets of the United States: From Paul Lawrence Dunbar to Langston Hughes (Urbana: University of Illinois Press, 1973), pp. 179-83. Johnson's work is also found in The Book of Negro Poetry, pp. 140-46; The Negro Caravan, pp. 347-48; and American Negro Poetry, pp. 25-27. James Weldon Johnson was not only poet and writer, but song composer, diplomat, civil rights executive and university professor. Among his poetic works are Fifty Years and Other Poems and God's Trombones.

Cromwell, editor, educator and historian, was a leading black spokesman between the 1870's and the first decades of the twentieth century. He authored in 1914, The Negro in American History. On Cromwell, see Meier, Negro Thought, pp. 44, 48, 50, 56, 94, 213, 261. Arthur A. Schomburg of black, Puerto Rican and Jewish ancestry, was a noted Negro bibliophile. His colection of books by and about black people is now a part of the New York Public Library System is its Schomburg Research Center of Black Culture. J.E. Bruce, a journalist and sometime editor, was president of the Negro Society for Historical Research. Meier, Negro Thought, pp. 262-63.

Williams was a noted heart surgeon and founder of Provident Hospital in Chicago. Moorfield Storey, as well as Villard and Ray Stannard Baker were white progressives whose support of black rights held steady during the nadir and its aftermath. Story and Villard were descendants of the nineteenth century Abolitionists. Baker was a leading muckraking journalist.

[71]The entire April, 1913 A.M.E. Review was devoted to the church and its ministry.

CHAPTER V

The Church: Locus of Social Christianity

(The Institutional Church and Social
Settlement) "It is a teaching,
ministering, nursing mother, and
seeks through its activities and
ministrations to level the
inequalties and bridge the chasm
between rich and poor, and the
educated and ignorant, the virtuous
and vicious, the indolent and the
thrifty, the vulgar and the refined,
and to bring all ages and classes of
the community to contribute to one
common good."[1]

Ransom's espousal of the Social Gospel was not essentially theoretical in derivation, but the result of his early pastoral experiences. It was during his pastorate at Manchester Mission, Allegheny City, Pennsylvania (1888-1890) that Ransom awakened to the urgent need for Social Chrisianity. He attested to this new awareness when he states,

> My first vision of the need for social
> service came to me as my wife and I
> almost daily went through the alleys
> and climbed the dark stairways of the
> wretched tenements, or walked out on
> the planks to the shanty boats where
> our people lived on the (Allegheny)
> river.[2]

The conditions described by Ransom were all too familiar in the lives of the masses of Blacks in the urban centers of the day. Employed in the most menial, yet backbreaking tasks, paid the lowest of wages, Blacks were forced to live in the poorest shanty-like housing which was generally located in unsafe and unhealthy neighborhoods. Many of the neighborhoods were often near railroad yards, canals, lakes, and river docks. Congestion, crime and disease were often rampant within these emerging slums.

Thousands of Blacks were employed by such companies as Diamond Steel, Midvale Steel and United States Steel. The black population of Pittsburg had grown from 1,115 in 1860 to 17,040 in 1900, an increase of more than 1,000 percent. Allegheny City's population was 3,315 when Ransom arrived in 1888.[3] Since Manchester Mission was located in a squalid section of the city, Ransom was exposed to urban poverty far more glaring than he had ever seen. It was because of that experience that Ransom realized that the church's role in society had to be expanded if the needs of people were to be met. Ransom was not only shocked by what he saw in Allegheny City, but disappointed also by what he did not find in Manchester Mision. He found only five members "worshipping in a reeking, alley-like street, in a small room containing three benches and some chairs."[4] the parish was at the lower end of the city bordering the river.

In two years Ransom built Manchester Mission into a thriving and growing congregation. Visiting his congregants wherever they lived, Ransom and his wife counselled them in their various crises and provided food and medicine for their illnesses through the church's benevolence fund. They also organized a Sunday School program to teach rudimentary education. By the time Ransom had completed his assignment at Manchester Mission, he had raised $6,000 and thereby constructed a new church. Many of Ransom's ideas, which later culminated in the Institutional Church and Social Settlement, were developed, nurtured and honed within this and other early pastoral assignments.

In 1893, Bishop Alexander Payne appointed Ransom to another urban congregation, Cleveland, Ohio's large and prestigious St. John's A.M.E. Church. During this appointment (1893-96) at St. John's A.M.E. Church, Cleveland's black population increased significantly. Blacks numbered about 6,000 which reflected an increase in twenty-five years of more than 400 percent. When Ransom assumed the pastorate of St. John's, it was Cleveland's largest black church. Within a year, partially as a result of the large migration of southern Blacks, more than 300 new names were added to that church's membership rolls.[5]

Reflecting the concerns and aspirations of St. John's membership for individual and group advancement, Ransom initiated a church program to respond to the needs of the total congregation. Again appropriating the methods of the Social Gospel, Ransom established such programs as infant classes, a kindergarten, a Boy's Christian Brigade, and a Junior Christian Endeavor Society. These efforts were directed toward the nurture and Christian development of children. Christian Endeavor, young men and women's auxiliaries and special youth programs were directed toward the adolescent and young adult populations. Men and women's clubs, the Men's Forum, the Board of Deaconesses, and the Women's Home Missionary Society were attempts to hold the interests of the adults within the congregation and the Tawawa Literary Society with its debates, lectures, recitals and speeches, transcended age and sex.[6]

Ransom's tenure at St. John's (1893-1896) was so succesful that his friend, Benjamin W. Arnett, who had been elevated to the episcopacy in 1888, assigned Ransom to yet another urban charge, Bethel A.M.E. Church in Chicago. When Ransom arrived at Bethel in 1896, Chicago was the second largest American city.

Sixty-eight percent of the city's population was foreign-born. Between 1890 and 1900, Chicago's black population more than doubled from 14,271 to 30,150. Only 19.8 percent of the black residents were born in Illinois, while 80.2 percent were born outside of the state. More significantly, 59 percent of the latter figure were born in the Southern and Border States.[7] Because of that growth, Bethel's membership also increased, making it the second largest A.M.E. Church in Chicago at the time.[8]

Three years later, according to the 1899 Minutes of the Iowa Conference, Bethel's full membership had increased 343 person, from 722 to 1,065.[9] Ransom did not flatter himself into believing that the standing-room only crowds at Bethel and its increasing membership were a result of his powerful pulpit oratory. He states,"...The chief contributing cause was not my preaching, but the fact that Chicago (was) filling up with Negroes from the South, brought there to work chiefly at the stock-yards and other industrial establishments."[10]

Under his leadership, Bethel attracted a number of the city's black professional and working-class inhabitants. Some of the upper-class Blacks who had attended Chicago's white churches prior to his arrival at Bethel, returned to the black church under Ransom's inspiring leadership. Thus, Ransom attracted both the educated and cultured as well as the unlearned and the unsophisticated. His success appears to have been related to his ability to speak with simple eloquence to the heads and hearts of his listeners, while challenging them to be actively involved in the issues of the day. Bethel's task, he said, was to "socialize itself so that it could become a vehicle for change in this world and in the world to come."[11]

Ida B. Wells, an active member of Bethel, described aspects of its varied activities to the Christian Recorder early in 1900. Ransom, she reported, had enlarged and broadened the church horizon by establishing certain innovative "auxiliary movements." She listed the Men's Sunday Club as an organization gathering young men off the streets and out of saloons to expose them to the city's very best professional and business representatives. The Men's Club met every Friday afternoon to discuss important topics of the day. A Women's Conference, she continued, had been organized along the same lines. Bethel Church, under Ransom's leadership, she went on, had established an industrial school for children, a kindergarten, and the Twentieth Century Club, a literary organization. The church, she concluded, was not concerned about its survival alone, but about the physical necessities of the people living in the district in which it was located.

Mrs. Wells reported that Ransom responded to the needs of the community by creating a board of twelve deaconesses "who cover that district seeking strangers, visiting the sick and feeding, clothing and making havens for the poor and needy."[12] Wells' article reveals her as an enthusiastic supporter and partisan of Ransom, and as one who believed that his ministry was innovative and visonary.

It appears that Ransom felt somewhat less sanguine about Bethel's accomplishments than did Wells. His aim was to develop an entirely new organization more ably suited to minister to the needs of Chicago's black populace. Through the influence of Bishop Arnett, who was president of the church's Financial Board, Ransom received the necessary funds to establish the Institutional Church and Social Settlement.

The Institutional Church and Social Settlement became the major structural medium through which he attempted to enact the influences of Jane Addams' Hull House and Graham Taylor's Social Settlement House, The Chicago Commons.[13] Conceptually, institutional churches borrowed the techniques they used from the Social Settlement Movement and endeavored to respond primarily to the moral, spiritual, social and industrial needs of European immigrants. Christian workers resided in the settlement buildings which most often adjoined the churches where numerous recreational, educational, and cultural programs occurred. By 1905, there were about seventy social settlements under the leadership of Christian groups around the country.[14] The primary manifestation of Ransom's combination of Social Gospel theory and racial consciousness was the Institutional Church and Social Settlement (ICSS) which he founded in Chicago in 1900.

When ICSS began in Chicago on July 22, 1900, there were approximately ten such institutions in that city. The significance of ICSS was the fact that it was the first organization of its kind in the United States owned and controlled by Blacks. Because of its uniqueness, ISCC was studied and observed by sociologists in the United States and in Europe. DuBois considered ICSS as "(the) most advanced step in the direction of making the church exist for the people rather than the people for the church." Ransom, in like manner, considered ICSS to be a Hull House or Chicago Commons founded by Blacks to help black people. Its aim was to help all needy persons whatever their race or creed, but its primary task was to reach the approximately 15,000 Blacks on Chicago's Southside as well as others arriving daily from the South.

Thus, at the age of 39, following 16 years of pastoring, Ransom had created ICSS for Blacks as the organizational apparatus most compatible with his theological commitment to racial and social uplift.[17] ICSS was formally inaugurated on October 21, 1900, and the foremeost representatives of the city's social settlement communities were in attendance. Addresses were delivered by Professor Graham Taylor of Chicago Commons and by Jane Addams of Hull Hourse. Addams also presented the fledgling institution with a $100 contribution. The assemblage was also addressed by Chicago Divinity School Professor, Shailer Matthews, then one of the nation's leading Social Gospel theorists.[18] In addition, the formal opening celebration was also addressed by three A.M.E. bishops: Abram Grant, presiding prelate of the district in which Institutional was located, Henry McNeal Turner, and Benjamin W. Arnett. Delegations representing A.M.E. Conferences from Indiana, Illinois and Iowa were also in attendance, and ICSS was filled to capacity with black Chicagoans of every social grouping. Thus, at ICSS, Ransom had brought together the disparate elements of Chicago's black community.[19]

It is significant that only a few years before, DuBois had castigated Philadelphia's black elite for failing to identify with and uplift its lower classes.[20] Therefore, Ransom;s Institutional Church was distinct since it provided upper-class Chicago Blacks an opportunity to serve the race. An example of this cross-section is in the fact that Institutional's Board of Managers reflected the city's black elite of the day. Its members included Dr. George G. Hall, S. Laing Williams, Edward H. Wright, Ferdinand L. Barnett and Dr. Daniel Hale Williams.[21]

The participation of Dr. and Mrs. Daniel Hale Williams at Institutional is illustrative of Ransom's ability and Institutional's program to attract members of the city's black upper-crust. The Ransoms had known Dr. Williams many years earlier when they pastored a church in the town of Hollidaysburg, Pennsylvania where Williams was born and raised. During their years in Chicago, the Ransoms considered Dr. Williams to have been their family physician.[22] Williams was probably the most prominent member of Chicago's black community. An outstanding surgeon who performed the first successful suture of the human heart, Williams moved freely between the city's white and black communities. Although members of a leading white Chicago congregation, he and his wife Alice were drawn to ICSS by its purpose and the revelance of its program and activities. Mrs. Williams became chairperson of a committee of prominent women organized to support and supervise various activities of its work. Ransom recalled that she was especially interested in Institutional's kindergarten and working mothers' programs.[23]

Although unable to participate as fully as he desired because of professional obligations, Dr. Williams attended ICSS Men's Sunday Evening Forum Series whenever he could. He met many friends at these gatherings which were organized to provide discussions of the important social, political and economic issues of the day affecting black Americans. Other young men, soon to distinguish themselves as leaders in the black community, attended the Men's Forum: L.B. Anderson, later Chicago alderman and State's Attorney; Edward H. Wright, at the time County Commisioner. Oscar DePriest, later to become Chicago's and the North's first black congressman, was also numbered among those who participated.[24]

Williams was enthusiastic about any institution that challenged people's mind and taught them to participate in the society in which they lived. Most probably, Williams admired Ransom as a minister because he did not preach about the hereafter, but preached about living and acting in the here and now.[25]

Along with other Social Gospelers of his day, Ransom was committed to the idea that the church sould help the community in its practical daily living by providing educational and recreational facilities for persons of all ages. Consistent with that belief, the Ransom family lived in the church Settlement House with two young seminarian associates, R.R. Wright (later an A.M.E. bishop) who was assistant pastor and ICSS Boy's Club director, and Monroe N. Work (later Tuskegee Institute's first Director of Research and Records), who assisted in the Boy's Club. Every aspect of the program, whether occurring during the day or night, was under the constant care and supervision of the staff.[26]

ICSS operated a day nursery where working mothers could leave their children during the day. A fully equipped gymnasium for men and women was open during the evenings, and classes in dressmaking, sewing, cooking and catering were held, as well as classes in voice, piano and choral study. Other activities included clubs for mothers, single women, boys and girls and a literary club, Christian Endeavor, and the Men's Sunday Evening Forum. ICSS also included a manual training department where young men were taught the printing trade. Ransom also established an Employment Bureau, furnishing cooks, maids, launderers, waiters, porters, butlers and stenographers to individuals and companies in need of such services. The employment service assisted persons in search of work.[27] While ICSS carried on the traditional church format of worship services, Wednesday night prayer meetings and the Home Missionary Society, its on-going program, combined elements of the industrial education program espoused by Booker T. Washington, and the program of finding employment for Negroes from the South advanced by the Committee on Social and Industrial Conditions of the Negro (later the National Urban League).

While many in Chicago and across the nation lauded the accomplishments of the Institutional Church and Social Settlement, such positive assessments were not universal. ICSS had hardly been formed before it encountered opposition. Ransom's fellow A.M.E. ministers, through their Chicago preacher's association, requested the presiding bishop, Abram Grant, to forbid him from preaching on Sundays except in the evening. Grant concurred with the request. The ministers feared that Ransom's popularity as a spell-binding preacher would compete with their regular Sunday morning worship services and draw their members to the new church. The ban was lifted some months later by the denomination's senior bishop, Henry McNeal Turner.[28] Despite Turner's action, the ministers continued their attacks on Ransom by forbidding their members from participating in any of the programs and activities at ICSS.[29] The opposition of his ministerial colleagues was the initial skirmish in a much larger and more intense struggle. At war were two groups with diametrically opposing views regarding not only the essence of the church, but what its mission in the world was to be. Ranoms' idea regarding Institutional was challenged by those within the denomination who accused him of establishing a settlement house rather than a church and neglecting the conventional religious commitment to the saving of souls.[30]

ICSS was "...not a church in the ordinary sense (but) a Hull House or Chicago Commons founded by Negroes for the help of people of that race." Ransom, on the other hand, contended that ICCS was a church, albeit the church of the future. ICSS, he wrote, "marked an epoch in the denominational life of the A.M.E. Church...Through the Institutional Church our connection (The A.M.E. Church) is stripping itself to enter the moral and spiritual race of the twentieth century."[31]

Ransom believed that the "future church" had to rethink its concept of membership in the new century if it was to attract a wider constituency. Thus, ICSS was not overly concerned about the denominational or doctrinal beliefs of its congregants and associates. While many socially concerned Chicagoans like Daniel Hale Williams were attracted to ICSS by its non-denominational flavor, many fervent A.M.E.'s found the non-denominational idea shocking and abhorrent.

Unlike his critics, Ransom believed that the church in urban America had to move beyond denominational particularity and traditional methods if its mission to black people was to be realized. The ICSS model, he argued in his first (and last) Quadrennial Report of Institutional Church, was the pattern for the future church. Ransom reported a membership of 306 persons and regular Sunday attendance approximating 800. Passionately, he wrote, "Many of those do not profess to be converted but have joined the church because of their interest in some of the department...(and) the spiritual life of the church (is) never more viorgorous."[32]

Othe prominent A.M.E. leaders did not share

110

Ransom's view of Institutional's vigorous spiritual life." H.T. Kealing, editor of the A.M.E. Review (1896-1912) clearly represented the opposing view. Writing in the January 1901 issue, Kealing suggested that the Institutional Church concept was a defensive method adopted by the Christian church with which to respond to changing circumstances. While affirming the positive aspects of the institutional churches, he perceived "danger lurking" in the background and warned that an over-emphasis on improving men's social environments might endanger the church's spiritual task of offering God's salvation to sinners. To Kealing, "The essential mission of the church has to be a witness for God, a weaning from sin and an invitation to regenerate lives."[33] Christian service, however laudatory, was considered by many like Kealing as secondary to the church's primary task of saving sinful souls. Kealing expressed the majority opinion of his fellow clergymen, white and black.

Tiring of the effort to justify ICSS, and forewarned that a plan had been initiated to replace him, Ransom abruptly left Chicago in 1904 for Massachusetts, where his friend, Bishop B. W. Arnett presided. Ransom recalled that his presiding Bishop, C. T. Shaffer, was under pressure to remove him from Institutional at the next Annual Conference. According to Ransom, he left the city before Bishop Shaffer could act. The minutes of the 1904 Iowa Annual Conference noted only that Ransom was transferred and stationed at New Bedford, Massachusetts. Ransom remained at the New Bedford Church just eight months before Bishop Arnett transferred him to the New England Conference's largest and most prestigious church, Charles Street A.M.E. Church in Boston.[34]

Many years later, Bishop R. R. Wright, Jr., who had served as one of Ransom's ministerial assistants at ICSS, recalled the reasons behind Ransom's transfer. According to Wright, the Reverend J. W. Townsend, the man assigned to succeed Ransom at ICSS, was appointed to "make ICSS a regular A.M.E. Church, to cut out the social foolishness and (to) bring religion back."[35] Institutional's nondenominational character was to be abolished. Indeed, by 1906, the Annual Conference journal reported that "the membership roll has been revised and tested to a point of truthfulness..." and perhaps as a further disavowal of Ransom's unorthodox policies, the report observed that "all the departments are healthy and being conducted according to the liking of the A.M.E. Church."[36]

Except for a brief paragraph in his _Autobiography_ concerning his transfer, Ransom has little to say on this matter, and for an individual who constantly wrote and spoke, it is a strange silence. The silence about the affair was broken forty years later in a letter Ransom wrote to Claude A. Barnett of the Associated Negro Press. Ransom stated that

> Most of the preachers of Negro churches of that day strenuously opposed it (the Institutional Church). It was entirely beyond their conception of what a church should be. Their only appeal was preaching, praying, singing, shouting, baptising and Holy Communion, but going out into the street and highways, bearing a message of social, moral, economic and civic salvation they did not believe to be a function of the church.[37]

Always an outspoken pastor, Ransom was disliked and envied by a number of his ministerial peers and was accused, perhaps justifiably, of not being a team player. Why he left Chicago in the manner in which he did is only partially understood. It can be surmised that he tired of the struggle between himself and his adversaries or that the responsibility of managing such an ambitious enterprise became too much for him. It is also feasible that the efforts to raise the monies to administer ICSS became for Ransom both physically and emotionally draining. On the other hand, when his opponents failed to grasp his vision or were threatened by his success, it is clear that they would not have rested until Ransom's Institutional Church had been defeated. Certainly, there were many who vehemently disagreed with thim theologically and ecclesiologically, and sought his removal. These opponents were committed to the rural-based "old-time" religion, while Ransom, a fervent proponent of the movement of southern Blacks to northern cities, believed that urbanization required new religious concepts and structures to serve the new migrants.

Despite his critics and detractors, Ransom believed that the Institutional Church concept had not been a failure, but that the A.M.E. Church had failed to grasp the importance of its existence as a paradigm for urban ministry. He knew from first-hand experience that the model was workable, since its basic framework had been constructed through the programs he had successfully developed in pastorates at Bethel, St. John's and Manchester Mission. Returning some years later to a modified ICSS model, Ransom established the church, Simon of the Cyrene (New York, 1913) where he again attempted to implement the basic concept of ICSS. This ministry at Simon of the Cyrene was primarily directed toward prostitutes and other undesirables. Thus Ransom continued to hold tenaciously to his belief in ICSS, which the following statement makes clear:

> Somehow, these two extremes--the Negro who is up and the Negro who is down, the Negro who is good and the Negro who is bad, the Negro who is intelligent and the Negro who is ignorant must be brought together until each stands uplifted....

The success accompanying Ransom's ministry came in large measure as the result of the loyal support and work of his second wife. They were a team during the early years of his career. Emma Ransom encouraged and stood by her husband's side as the patterns of his ministry developed. Some years after Emma's death, Ransom wrote,

> For 55 years we travelled over the country together, accepting each new assignment with renewed courage and vigor. Together we combed the alleys and dark passageways, hoping to bring spiritual guidance to our people living in the wretched tenements and miserable hovels. Together we begged funds to foster innovations in the church, and together we offered comfort to those who occasionally slipped from grace.[38]

Emma Ransom was a co-worker who assisted her husband in organizing Sunday schools, kindergartens, and youth groups at each church appointment. She encouraged and led efforts to introduce the congregants to black spirituals as well as classical compositions. Under her guidance, the churches became known for the excellence of their choral music. Like her spouse, Emma was deeply interested in literature and literary pursuits. Under her impetus, the Tawawa Literary Society flourished.

The society sponsored forums and debates in many on subjects and was responsible for engaging such noted speakers as the militant anti-lynching crusader, Ida B. Wells and the young poet, Paul Laurence Dunbar.[39]

Similar to her husband, Emma's interest extended to the issue of missions. Perhaps because their early pastoral assignments had occurred in expanding albeit squalid industrial towns in the Northeast and Midwest, Emma was also particularly sensitive to the needs of the newly arrived black urban migrants. As a result, she became as early supporter and participant in a denominational organization which was primarily concerned with southern migrants--the Women's Parent Mite and Missionary Society (WPMMS). The society's first annual convention in 1894 was held at St. John's A.M.E. Church which was pastored at that time by her husband. In three subsequent pastorates, Emma Ransom founded similar local societies.[40]

WPMMS was founded in 1874 and endorsed in 1876 by the General Conference. The society was the direct result of pressure applied by the A.M.E. women for broader participation within the denomination. The women insisted that the General Conference accord WPMMS the same status and recognition given to other major auxiliaries within the church. Thus, WPMMS was the first women's group to be officially recognized and accepted as a complete department within the A.M.E. Church. The Society's purpose was to assist the denomination's Missionary Department in the formation of local missionary societies throughout the General Church and to raise funds to foster its missionary activities at home and abroad.[41] Through WPMMS, the missionary program of the church was strengthened and enlarged. By recognizing the Society and providing it specific duties, the church accomodated female demands for more significant involvement, while maintaining male power and control.

In 1896, Emma Ransom became president of the WPMMS, which she had organized at Bethel A.M.E. Church. Under her leadership, the Society not only initiated and implemented projects to aid indigent persons and families within the Chicago community, but also consistently raised more money for missions than any other church within the Iowa Conference.

The wider Chicago community was served by Bethel's

114

outreach program, and the denominational program was supported as well. The Presiding Elder of the Iowa Conference lauded Mrs. Ransom's work when he wrote:

> Mrs. R. C. Ransom is justly entitled to share the honors for Bethel's splendid success, for she has been a faithful helper to her husband, thus endearing herself to the members who say she has excelled all her predecessors in her many works of helpfulness to the church. She has succeeded in interesting the women in mission work to a point where instead of reporting nothing as formerly, they report this year over one hundred dollars mite missionary monies. [42]

By 1898, Emma had become the First Vice President of the Iowa Conference's Women's Mite Missionary Society. She would be involved as a Society leader at the local and national level for the next forty years. [43]

Clearly Emma convinced that women had a unique role was to play in the life of the church. She expressed that conviction by publishing, with another A.M.E. minister's wife, a women's missionary magazine, <u>Women's Light and Love for Africa</u>. This publication was the first and largest missionary journal published by the A.M.E. denomination. [44] Ransom recalled that the primary inspiration for the magazine came as a result of the visit made by a group of South African singers to America. The group had been brought to perform at the World's Columbian Exposition and to tour the country. Following the Exposition, the performers travelled as far as Cleveland, where they were stranded and deserted by their sponsor. The Ransoms heard about their situation and sheltered them with the help of St. John's Women's Missionary Society. The South Africans desired higher education. However, when their matriculation at Howard University could not be arranged, the Ransoms appealed to Bishop Benjamin Arnett, who was at the time Chairman of the Trustee Board at Wilberforce.

Bishop Arnett agreed to accpet all of them at Wilberforce University. When two of the students graduated from Wilberforce and returned to South Africa, they distinguished themselves as pioneer A.M.E. missionaries and educators. [45]

Women's Light and Love for Africa was a way for Emma to express her conviction that women had been called to Christian service just as men had been. Unfortunately, the magazine's circulation was too small and the church was not ready for it; as a consequence, the magazine folded.

Emma's effort to expand the areas of opportunity for female expression within the A.M.E. Church was consistent with the efforts made by women in other American denominations. These Christian women were troubled by the dislocations in the society and genuinely wished to do their part in alleviating those problems. With urbanization, industrialization and the resumption of large-scale immigration after the Civil War, human suffering became endemic and as historian Janet Wilson James notes,

> Familes (were) broken by privation and unemployment, leaving orphaned children, rootless young, the helpless, sick, and aged...The physical deprivation of the poor seemed inseparable from their spiritual needs; the relief effort took on the proportions of a religious crusade.[46]

With this special concern for the family, the home and the church, Christian women desired to join their men in the "crusade" to re-make American society.

Generally, the male-dominated church hierarchies were less than enthusiastic toward the urgings of women for broader church participation. Even when deaconess orders and women's missionary societies were approved, men imposed financial controls upon them. Majority male opinion believed that the women's place was in the home. Thus, some women sought and found increased opportunities for service and control in nondenominational agencies such as the Women's Christian Temperance Union (WTCU) and the Young Women's Christian Association (YWCA). Other women, like Emma Ransom, refused to compartmentalize their concerns and continued the roles of homemaker, church worker and club participant. Emma's denominational and nondenomational activities can be best understood when placed within that historical context.

During the late 1880's, the pages of the A.M.E.

Review reflected the growing debate within church circles regarding the role of women in church and society. Most of the articles written by males deplored women's attempts to foresake their God-given duties as preservers of the home and urged them to remember the various Biblical injunctions that affirmed that role.[47] Emma did not dispute or deny the primacy of women's role as homemakers, but nevertheless supported their efforts toward broader community involvements.

She not only committed her life to a shared ministry with her husband in the church, but was involved in social and civic organizations as well. An active club woman, she was considered a gifted speaker and organizer whose talents were used in numerous organizations, among them being the National Association of Colored Women's Clubs, and the Women's Christian Temperance Union. Emma was president of the local WCTU during the years she and her husband were in Cleveland. She was also active in the Young Women's Christian Assoction and during her husband's pastorate of Bethel A.M.E. Church in New York City (1907-1912) served as chairman of the Board of Management of New York's "Colored YWCA." She was particularly concerned about providing necessary shelter and assistance for the large number of females migrating from the South. Thus, Emma chaired a drive to raise the necessary funds to build a residence in which black southern women could be housed when they arrived in the city. The fundraising effort was successful and the YWCA building, constructed in Harlem, was named the Emma S. Ransom House.[48]

Despite such civic involvements, or perhaps because of them, Emma constantly affirmed her belief that home and hearth were women's basic responsibilities. Aware that many of those who lamented the expanding role of women were her husband's ministerial colleagues, she endeavored to blunt their sharpest criticisms. This she accomplished by cautioning women that participation in racial and social betterment organizations could be a "positive harm" if they caused women to become restive and dissatisfied. Organizational activity was more than justified and a powerful aid to family and race development, "if the energy and investment required for participation in clubs and other groups give women the strength to return to our homes and better grapple with the problems there,"[49] she stressed. Addressing the 1905 Convention of the Northeastern Federation of Women's Clubs in a speech entitled "The Home-Made Girl,"

117

Emma declared that the family was the oldest and most sacred of institutions established by God. Schools, clubs, public libraries, and the church were necessary to the development of womanhood, but the home was the arena for the building of character, refinement, and the social graces. The home was the training ground for future mothers in whose hands the coming generation would be placed. "Woman has no greater title and high goal than marriage and motherhood," she stated.[50] Thus, Emma's activist posture must be interpreted as her way of fulfilling her Christian responsibilities. She and others like here were not feminists, but women who basically accepted the church's traditional and conservative appellation of them as the "bearers of Christianity and civilization." What she and they refused to accept were the limitations male assigned to that role. Emma and her husband shared the conviction that women were central to the church's realization of its mission to society.

Late in 1894, while pastoring St. John's A.M.E. Church in Cleveland, Ransom organized and consecrated the first Board of Deaconesses in the A.M.E. Church. It was his sense of the times, the needs of the people, and Emma's involvement in civic and religious matters that led him to that decision. Ransom also established a deaconess board during his pastorate at Bethel A.M.E. Church in Chicago. Twelve deaconesses were assigned to various essential community tasks. Furthermore, the ministry of Bethel was extended to the unchurched of the Chicago Southside.[51] Thus, Ransom not only responded to the yearnings of women for increased responsibilities and recognition as Christian workers, but institutionalized within Bethel Church a group expressive of those wishes. It is also evident that Ransom considered the deaconness board as a useful ally in his attempts to broaden the outreach capabilities of Bethel Church.

An incident at Bethel gives further insight into Ransom's position on women's service within the church. One of Bethel's members, Sarah Slater, had been ordained a deaconess by Chicago's white Methodist Epsiscopal Bishop. Slater had completed the course equipping her for foreign and home mission service at the deaconess training institution in that city. As a pastor of Bethel, Ransom accepted and recognized her training and competence. Slater had been paid by the Methodist Episcopal Church for her years of training and service at the Methodist Hospital, but as a member of Bethel, she desired to use her expertise on behalf of the race.

Writing in the 1898 <u>A.M.E. Christian Recorder</u>, Ransom asked the A.M.E. Church to recognize not only Slater's deaconess orders, but to approve the designation of women as deacons throughout the denomination. He expressed the prevailing stereotypic rational and defense of that request when he stated

> It is conceded that there are certain kinds of work in the church which women can do better than men; a deaconness is a minister of the church called upon to exercise her special gift of teaching, nursing, or whatever it may be in the service of the church for the purpose of extending the Kingdom of the Lord Jesus...The gentle ministry of women in the church is, I think, more in keeping with their sex, the tenet of Scripture, and the needs of the times...A condition, not a theory, led me to write this.[52]

Ransom's point of view is clearly that of a supportive Social Gospeler. His strong support of the deaconess as an accredited church worker and his proposal that her "gentle ministry...is more in keeping with her sex" is case in point.[53] Confronted by those who contended that women's place was in the home, it is possible that some Social Gospelers did not reject that contention, but broadened it by insisting that women were uniquely compassionate and that they would humanize the ministry of the church as they humanized the home.

Ransom's query regarding the deaconess issue was answered two years later in 1900 when the church, during its Twenty-First General Conference, authorized the Office of Deaconess. However, its recognition was only a partial victory for women, since deaconesses were not accorded clerical status, but designated instead as ministerial aides and helpers.[54]

Ransom's support of an expanding role for women in the church was not confined to deaconesses, but to women who aspired to the ministry as well. During his pastorate at North Street A.M.E. Church in Springfield, Ohio, Ransom welcomed to the pulpit such an aspirant,

the black evangelist, Amanda Smith. Convinced of her
call to God's service and rebuffed in her attempts to
enter the ordained ministry, Amanda Smith entered the
field of evangelism. She travelled, nationally and
internationally, proclaiming the gospel message. An
admirer and friend of Smith, Ransom served on the Board
of Managers of the Illinois Orphan Home she
founded.[55] In a tribute written soon after her death in
1914, Ransom remembered her as being a "clear-minded
prophetess" who saw deliverance from present oppression
as clearly as she had foretold emancipation from
slavery.

> Her legacy to the race was her trust in
> God and her belief that racial salvation
> lay in temperance, social service,
> holiness, and the rescue of neglected
> children.[56]

Ransom's estimation of the role women played in the
betterment of society was not limited to the church. As
a participant in many organizations and institutions,
particularly in Cleveland and Chicago during the 1890's,
Ransom was aware that many of those organizations were
sustained and maintained by the tireless efforts of
women. He was associated with prominent club leaders:
Mary Church Terrell and Fannie B. Williams; Social
Settlement leaders such as Jane Addms of Hull House, and
Mary McDowell of the Chicago University Settlement; the
educator Fanny Jackson Coppin, and the crusading
journalist and activist, Ida B. Wells.[57] Wells and
Ransom met during the World Columbian Expostion in 1893.
A lone, but powerfully effective fighter against
lynching, she was national president of the
Anti-Lynching League. She brought her organization's
message to Cleveland's St. John's A.M.E. Church in 1894
under the sponsorship fo the Tawawa Literary Society. A
local chapter of the Anti-Lynching League was formed
soon afterwards and Reverdy C. Ransom was elected its
president. When the Ransoms arrived in Chicago two
years later to pastor Bethel A.M.E. Church, Ida B. Wells
was one of their most active parishioners. Ransom held
her in high esteem and respected Well's courage and
persistent militance in the crusade against lynching.
They had travelled many roads together, he stated,
"through the wet of the storm and the rain and the mire,
seeking to speak and plead with men of power to use
their influence to aid the Negroes' cause."[58] Speaking
before the Ida B. Wells Club, Ransom applauded Ida B.

Wells and her groups for their efforts in the areas of prison reform, family hygiene, educational reform, child care, and civil rights. He noted that they and women like themselves were actively engaged in the greater and larger questions of the time, taking their place side by side with their men. They were an example of a new departure and should be honored, especially for their work in the city of Chicago.[59] The 1890's was a period when women's clubs multiplied in the city and nationwide. These early groups became the nucleus for the Federated Women's Clubs that followed.

Ransom was also determined that the church's urban outreach program included women. With the assistance of his wife and Wells, Ransom organized at Bethel A.M.E. Church the Women's Conference, which was the church's effort to recruit young women away from the evils of the streets and to provide them with a healthy environment in which they could gather to discuss and share their common concerns. Believing in character development and the necessity of proper role models, the Ransoms made certain that the young women were exposed to Christian values. The Women's Conference convened every Friday afternoon and the topics discussed included proper hygiene, child care, home-making, and Christian family living.[60] This stress on family life was particularly urgent as juvenile delinquency increased within the society.

Social Gospelers, increasingly aware of the rapid movement of population from the country to the city, and the secularization of the public schools and the numerous temptations of city life, looked to the Sunday School to inculate moral values within children. In like manner, Ransom believed that with guidance during their formative years, children would grow to become church-going and respectable members of society. THe very first effort Reverdy and Emma undertook during their early pastoral appointments was the establishment of Sunday schools. Emma spearheaded these efforts, and also recruited and trained the teachers. She used many of the excellent manuals developed primarily by the Chautauqua movement for their training. The Ransoms' commitment to children is evident, since they organized kindergartens, created children's day programs, and developed special Sunday worship services.[61] Since both Emma and her husband were aware of the new organizational techniques used to attract children, especially pre-adolescent boys, they established a boys' group called the Ransom Cadets in 1895 at St. John's Church in Cleveland, and again during their pastorate at the Bethel Church in Chicago.[62] The Cadets were patterned after the United Boys' Brigade, founded by W. A. Smith of the Free College Church of Glasgow. Ransom's cadet program stressed compulsory attendance at Sunday school and weekly meetings for Bible drill. The United Boys' Brigade began in 1883 and spread rapidly throughout Europe. By 1890, the first American Brigade appeared in a San Franciso church. By 1895, there were 1,000 Brigade chapters in the United States with a membership of 25,000.[63] The Brigades were yet another example of Social Gospel ferment.[64] Thus, the Sunday schools, kindergartens, and brigades established by Emma and Ransom were successful. Similarly, Ransom, fearing that many young people would be irretrievably lost to the church during their teenage years, established programs for adolescents, and youth auxiliaries which were in fact Social Gospel groups.

Ransom had entered the ministry during the period when youth work within the A.M.E. Church was just beginning, and he became an early proponent of the Epworth League and Christian Endeavor Societies.[65] In 1891, while pastoring the North Street A.M.E. Church in Springfield, Ohio, Ransom organized an extremely successful Epworth League,[66] and at St. John A.M.E. Church in Cleveland, he organized a United Society of Christian Endeavor. St. John's was host to a Christian Endeavor Convention in 1894. The young people's choir of the church sang during the meeting, and Ransom was responsible for the delegates' housing and accomodations. The Gazette commended him for the "splendid manner" in which the entire convention was organized and conducted. Because of his involvement with young people in the local and general church, Ransom was delegated with others to represent the A.M.E. denomination in 1897 at the national Christian Endeavor Convention in San Francisco.[67] The Epworth League and Christian Endeavor were both expressions of the Social Gospel in action.

Ransom's interest in these societies pre-dated their recognition by the A.M.E. Denomination, since it was not until 1896 that the A.M.E. General Conference recognized local Christian societies as official youth groups. By an action of the 1900 General Conference, these groups were formed into a church-wide or connectional society named the Allen Christian Endeavor

League. The major objectives of the Allen Christian Endeavor League, in keeping with the historic goals of the United Society of Christian Endeavor were, "to promote intelligent and practical Christian living among the young...to train them in the proper methods of Christian work and helpfulness...(and) to strengthen and purify the social life of our young people."68 Such aims were central facets of Ransom's life-long concern for youth and his convictions were widely shared by late nineteenth century Protestantism.

The years and activities of Ransom's pastoral ministry (1884-1912) were tumultous ones in American religious history. Faced with the enormity of change occurring in the society, a significant minority of clergy and laity believed that the church was obligated, if not theologically destined, to play a central role in the process of social justice and social amelioration. The contour of Ransom's ministry reflects his acceptance of the aforementioned premise whether one notes his enthusiasm for Social Gospel organizations or his advocacy, along with his wife, of the broadened participation of women in the church and society. He was extremely receptive to the ideas and techniques of the Social Gospel Movement and implemented many of its organizational concepts in the churches he pastored. That he was aware of and willing to experiment with the newer forms of ministry is evident in his establishment of chapters of the Epworth League, the United Society of Christian Endeavor, the United Boys' Brigade, and his culminating achievement, the founding of the Institutional Church and Social Settlement. Thus, Ransom synthesized the various expressions of the Social Gospel into his own innovative concept of ministry. Ransom sought through the mechanism of Institutional Church to respond to the times and the needs of black city dwellers. He wrote:

> The Institutional A.M.E. Church of Chicago was not born before its time. It comes to meet and serve the social condition and industrial need of the people, and to give answers and solutions to the many grave problems which confront our Christianity in the great centers of population of our people...69

Footnotes

[1]Ransom, "The Institutional Church," Christian, Recorder, March 7, 1901, p.1

[2]Ransom, Pilgrimage, p. 49.

[3]Richard R. Wright, The Negro in Pennsylvania: A Study in Economic History (1912, rpt. New York: Arno Press & New York Times, 1968), pp. 93-94, 222, 228.

[4]Ransom, Pilgrimage, p. 47.

[5]Gerber, Black Ohio, pp. 145, 274; Davis, Black American in Cleveland, p. 186. The influx of black migrants was so great that Ransom helped establish, in another section of Cleveland, the St. James A.M.E. Church. Dedication, Souvenir Edition, St. James A.M.E. Church, April 1953, p. 3; Ransom Papers, Wilberforce University Archives; Gazette, September 29, 1894, p. 3; Ransom, Pilgrimage, p. 69.

[6]Gazette, February 10, 1894, April 7, 1894, May 19, 1894, November 24, 1894, December 1, 1894, December 2, 1894.

[7]St. Clair Drake, "Churches and Voluntary Associations in the Negro Community," Report of Official Project 465-54-3-386, Works Progress Administration (Chicago, 1940), p. 86; Allan H. Spear, Black Chicago: The Making of a Negro Ghetto, 1890-1920 (Chicago: The University of Chicago Press, 1967), pp. 11-12.

[8]Spear, Black Chicago, pp. 91-93.

[9]Statistical Tables, The Fourteenth, Sixteenth and Seventeenth Sessions of the Iowa Annual Conference, September 1896, 1898, 1899.

[10]Ransom, Pilgrimage, p. 82.

[11]Ransom, "The Industrial and Social Conditions of the Negro," p. 9, Wilberforce University Archives; "Confessions of a Bishop," Ebony, p. 79.

[12]Ida Wells Barnett, "Reverend R. C. Ransom, B.D. "Christian Recorder, January 1, 1898.

[13]Ransom, *Pilgrimage*, p. 104.

[14]Hopkins, *The Rise of the Social Gospel*, pp. 154-56.

[15]DuBois, "The Negro Church," p. 85; Bucke, *History of Methodism*, pp. 552-53.

[16]*Inter-Ocean*, July 29, 1900.

[17]*Inter-Ocean*, July 29, 1900.

[18]Ransom, "The Institutional Church," *Recorder*, March 7, 1901, p. 2.

[19]Ransom, "The Institutional Church," p. 2.

[20]DuBois, *The Philadelphia Negro*, pp. 392-93.

[21]*Inter-Ocean*, July 29, 1900.

[22]Blockson, *Pennsylvania's Black History* (Philadelphia: Portfolio Associates, Inc., 1975), p. 47; Ransom, *Pilgrimage*, p. 44; Helen Buckler, *Doctor Dan*, p. 224.

[23]Helen Buckler to Reverdy C. Ransom, January 26, 1945; Ransom to Helen Buckler, February 21, 1945; Daniel Hale Williams Collection Howard University, Moorland-Spingard Research Center; Helen Buckler, *Doctor Dan - Pioneer in American Surgery* (Boston: Little Brown & Co., 1954), p. 222.

[24]Buckler, *Doctor Dan*, p. 225; Wright, *87 Years*, pp. 95-96; Ransom, *Pilgrimage*, p. 116.

[25]Buckler, *Doctor Dan*, p. 271.

[26]Wright, *87 Years*, p. 94; *Pilgrimage*, p. 91; Burkett & Newman, *Black Apostles*, p. 197; *The Negro Handbook*, compiled by the Editors of *Ebony* (Chicago: Johnson Publishing Co., 1966), p. 104.

[27]Ransom, "First Quadrennial Report, the Institutional Church," n.p.; Ransom Papers, Wilberforce University Archives; Spear, *Black Chicago*, pp. 95-96; Wright, *87 Years*, p. 194; *The Inter-Ocean*, July 29, 1900; *The Christian Recorder*, November 29, 1900.

[28]Ransom, _Pilgrimage_, p. 111; Wright, _87 Years_, p. 94.

[29]Ransom, _Pilgrimage_, pp. 111-12; Spear, _Black Chicago_, p. 95.

[30]Florette, Henri, _Black Migration: Movement North, 1900-1920_ (New York: Anchor Books, 1976), p. 187.

[31]_Christian Recorder_, November 29, 1900, p. 2; Ransom, "The Institutional Church."

[32]Buckler, _Doctor Dan_, p. 224; Ransom, "The Institutional Church," n.p.; "First Quadrennial Report, Institutional Church," n.p.

[33]H.T. Kealing, "Editorial, The Institutional Church," _A.M.E. Review_, January, 1901, p. 87.

[34]Minutes, Twenty-Second Iowa Annual Conference, September, 1904, p. 20; Wright, _87 Years_, pp. 99; Ransom, _Pilgrimage_, pp. 135, 143-48.

[35]Wright, _87 Years_, p. 148.

[36]Minutes, Thirty-Fifth Sessions, Illinois Conference, September, 1906, p. 31.

[37]Ransom to Claude A. Barnett, May 14, 1945; Claude A. Barnett Papers, Chicago Historical Society

[38]Ransom, "Confessions of a Bishop," _Ebony_, p. 74.

[39]_Gazette_, Oct. 27, 1894, Dec. 1, 1894, Dec. 12, 1896; Davis, _Black American in Cleveland_, p. 122; _Pilgrimage_, p. 60.

[40]_Gazette_, May 19, 1894, June 30, 1894; _Minutes, Fifteenth Session Iowa Annual Conference_, 1897, p. 39; _Seventeenth Session, Iowa Annual Conference_, 1899, pp. 35, 50.

[41]Wills, "Aspects of Social Thought," p. 171.

[42]_Seventeenth Session Iowa Annual Conference_, 1899, p. 35.

[43]_Sixteenth Session Iowa Annual Conference_, 1898,

126

pp. 32-33; L.L. Berry, A Century of Missions of the A.M.E. Church (New York: Gutenberg Printing Co., Inc., 1942), p. xi.

[44]Gazette, January 20, 1984.

[45]Berry, A Century of Missions, pp. 158, 186-87; Walter L. Williams, "Ethnic Relations of African Students in the United States with Black Americans, 1870-1900," Journal of Negro History, 65, (Summer, 1980), pp. 231-32; R.R. Wright, Jr. 87 Years Behind the Black Curtain, pp. 226-27; Wright, Bishops, p. 82.

[46]Janet Wilson James, ed., Women in American Religion (Philadelphia: University of Pennsylvania Press, 1980), p. 9.

[47]Wills, "Social Aspects," pp. 162-66.

[48]Review, January 1914, pp. 246-48; Wright, Bishops, p. 291; Ransom, Pilgrimage, pp. 203-4.

[49]Emma S. Ransom, "The Home-Made Girl," n.p.; Ransom Papers, Payne Theological Seminary Archives.

[50]Emma S. Ransom, "The Home-Made Girl," n.p.

[51]Ida B. Wells Barnett, "Reverend R. C. Ransom, B.D."; Recorder, Jan. 25, 1900, p. 1.

[52]Christian Recorder, July 14, 1898.

[53]Christian Recorder, July 14, 1898.

[54]Wills, "Aspects of Social Thought," pp. 185-91.

[55]Gazette, July 15, 1893, p. For further information on Amanda Smith, see An Autobiography of Mrs. Amanda Smith, the Colored Evangelist (Chicago: Meyer and Brothers Publishers, 1893).

[56]Ransom, "Editorial, Amanda Smith," Review, April, 1915, pp. 405-7. Smith's picture adorned the Review's front cover.

[57]Ransom, Pilgrimage, p. 88; Spear, Black Chicago, p. 63.

[58]Ransom, "Deborah and Jael," pp. 5-7; Ransom

Papers, Payne Theological Seminary Archives; Pilgrimage, p. 117.

[59]Ransom, "Deborah and Jael," p. 7.

[60]Ida Wells Barnett, "R. C. Ransom, B. D. "Christian Recorder, January 25, 1900, p. 1.

[61]The Gazette, November 25, 1893, March 31, 1894, June 9, 1894.

[62]The Gazette, June 6, 1896.

[63]Abell, The Urban Impact on American Protestantism, pp. 208-09.

[64]Abell, The Urban Impact, pp. 210-11.

[65]Abell, The Urban Impact, pp. 212-14.

[66]The Wilberforce Alumnal, December, 1891, p. 26.

[67]Gazette, June 30, July 7, 1894; J.W. Beckett, "Our Trip to Christian Endeavor," Christian Recorder, August 26, 1897, pp. 6, 1.

[68]Bucke, History of Methodism, 2, pp. 544-45.

[69]Ransom, "The Institutional Church," Christian Recorder, March 7, 1901, p. 1

CHAPTER VI

Power, Politics and Social Realities

The traitors within the ranks of our race are known. They have neither our confidence nor our hearts. What standing they have is due to the powerful support which is given them by misguided men of wealth, by politicians who for personal or partisan advantage would use them to profit by the vanishing remnants of the Negro's political power, and by a newspaper press whose approving voice is the mouthpiece of a decadent public opinion, which would let the Negro question "work itself out" under the baneful influence of the many degrading forms of Jim Crowism.[1]

As the nineteenth century ended and the twentieth century began, Blacks had begun to lose those civil and political rights they had won during the Civil War and Reconstruction. The Compromise of 1877 was indicative of that ominous trend. In the name of sectional peace and economic development between the North and South, the Republican Party agreed to withdraw the last remaining federal troops from the South. Orginally, those soldiers had been sent there to protect the rights of the freedmen, particularly their voting rights.[2] Although disfranchisement occurred manifestly under varying circumstances, by the 1890's and early 1900's Blacks had been virtually excluded from participation in southern political life. This right to vote was denied by numerous legal techniques, among which were the poll tax, the grandfather clause, literacy tests, and white primaries.[3] Furthermore, Supreme Court decisions during what Rayford Logan has called the "nadir," reflected the nations' eroding commitment to black rights. In 1883, the Court invalidated the Civil Rights Act of 1875--the Court action which undermined the civil and political rights engendered by the 14th and 15th amendments. In 1896, through its Separate But Equal ruling in the Plessey vs. Ferguson decision, the Court gave legal sanction to segregation. Thus, as the twentieth century began, Blacks found themselves abandoned by former friends and allies and subject to segregation, intimidation and violence. Lynching was commonplace in the South and anti-black riots occurred in cities throughout the country. The question faced by Ransom and his contemporaries concerned the development of effective strategies to counter and reverse their people's deteriorating condition within American society.

Two major strategies emerged during the twenty years between 1895 and 1915. Both "conservative" and "radical" groups, as they became known,[4] asserted that their approaches were the best prescriptions for racial advancement and progress. These antagonists shared certain related assumptions. Both acknowledged the debilitating effects of slavery on the race and were acutely aware of the obstacles preventing its advancement within the society. These leaders therefore urged Blacks to prepare themselves for eventual admission into full American citizenship. Exemplifying nineteenth century America's presumptions that individuals as well as racial groups would triumph over the vagaries of life if they possessed character, determination and will, these spokesmen challenged Blacks to become self-sufficient, to acquire the habit of thrift and hard work, and to lead moral and upright lives. They also believed that the primary responsibility for racial uplift would come from the strivings of black people themselves. A speech given by Reverdy Ransom in Boston's Faneuii Hall in 1909, supports the above viewpoint. The occasion was the fiftieth anniversary of the execution of John Brown. Suggesting that Blacks had to present their case for equal opportunity and equal justice to the great jury of the American people, Ransom said, "We must do it (present the case) by industry and thrift, by honesty and sobriety, by enterprise and energy, by intelligence and character, by demonstrating our capacity and displaying our ability, by patriotism and courage, and by taking our place in the ranks of men without losing step with the march of progress."[5] Yet, despite the similarities of their racial ends, the two opposing groups were at odds when the question of means was raised.

Concurring that the conflict was one of means and not ends, Kelly Miller, one of America's most prominent black intellectuals of that day, observed that "Radical and Conservative Negroes agree to the end in view, but differ as to the most effective means of attaining it. The difference is not essentially one of the principle or purpose, but point of view."[6] Miller might have observed as well that a crucial difference between the two groups involved one group's access to powerful and wealthy Whites and the other's inability to get a hearing from them.

The most influential black leader of the period was Booker T. Washington, prinicpal of Tuskegee and foremost advocate of Industrial education for Blacks. Washington's racial strategy and philosophy were most consonant with white opinion of the times, and he received generous white support, and with the aid was able to achieve enormous power within America. Although Washington publicly deprecated attempts by Blacks to acquire the franchise and political power, privately he commanded enormous political influence as the link between the black community and the white political establishment. Prior to their appointments, most black aspirants for political favor were first approved by the "Wizard from Tuskegee."[7] Washington's political power spanned the Republican Administrations of William McKinley, Theodore Roosevelt, and William Howard Taft

(1896-1912). He displayed similar acumen in his
relationships with the great industrialists of the day.
Washington was a close friend of William H. Baldwin,
Jr., vice president of the Southern Railroad and later
president of the Long Island Railroad, and he persuaded
Baldwin to become a trustee and eventually chairman of
Tuskegee's board of trustees. Washington also numbered
among his numerous wealthy advisors and benefactors, the
railroad   magnate,   Collis   P.   Huntington,   the
industrialist Andrew Carnegie, and Standard Oil's
founder and president, John D. Rockefeller. These and
other leaders of American philanthrophy rarely
contributed to black causes or organizations without
first seeking Washington's advice and counsel. Because
of his access to such financial and political resources,
Washington was able to underwrite, and in some cases,
virtually run and control major black newspapers of the
times.   He also encouraged or discouraged black
educators from seeking philanthropic aid for their
struggling institutions, or assistance for their
research projects, and aided or blocked those persons
who sought political appointment. Thus, the struggle
between the radicals and the conservatives also involved
the power of Booker T. Washington and his "Tuskegee
Machine" to set the agenda for black America.[8]   The
radicals espoused the tactic or protest and the
immediate receipt of what they considered fundamental
manhood rights: protection from lynch-law, equal
justice, the right to vote, and the right to
employment.[9]

Washington's   strategy   of   accommodation   was
essentially one of conciliation and gradualism,
believing as he did, that prejudice and discrimination
resulted from the ignorance and poverty of Blacks
themselves. Blacks, not the Whites, were to blame for
the abject condition. Thus, to Washington, Blacks bore
the major responsiblity for their own elevation.   He
contended that Blacks would eventually prove themselves
worthy of white respect by acquiring thrift, industry
and Christian character, and insisted that it would be
through economic accumulation and moral uprightness that
Blacks would achieve white acceptance and thereby alter
their staus. Washington believed that the South, where
the vast majority of Blacks lived at the time, was the
primary place where black economic advancement was to be
attained, and stated that black people had no better
friends than southern Whites.   He believed that by
remaining on the land and by acquiring the education and
skills appropriate to farming and other agricultural

132

pursuits, black advancement would be assured. Furthermore, he advocated agricultural and industrial training for the black southern masses and considered the emphasis on training Blacks for the professions as largely irrelevant and unnecessary.[10] However, it was Washington's seeming acceptance of segregation, his silence on lynching, and his public criticism of (and private efforts to silence) those who advocated black political participation that most incensed his radical critics, one of whom was Reverdy C. Ransom. If, as August C. Meier suggests, most radicals were drawn from the ranks of college-educated professional men who were born and raised in the North, Ransom's background fits that general description.[12]

When Booker T. Washington delivered his famous Atlanta Exposition address in 1895, Ransom was pastoring in Cleveland, Ohio. Among his many civic activities was his leadership of an Anti-Lynching Committee, which had been established there following a visit of the anti-lynching crusader, Ida B. Wells. Thus, while Booker T. Washington remained silent regarding the rising incidents of lynching across the South, Wells, Ransom, and others were deploring such incidents and agitating that Blacks be protected and that their white assailants be apprehended and punished. Cleveland at the time was a center of opposition to Booker T. Washington. The opposition was led by Harry C. Smith, publisher of the city's widely read black newspaper, The Gazette. Smith was persistent and caustic in his criticism of the Washington philosophy.

Ransom and Smith worked together on the Anti-Lynching Committee and shared membership in other protest organizations. Smith was founder of the Afro-American League, a charter member of the Niagara Movement, and a member of the NAACP's Select Committee of One Hundred.[13] A liberal and essentially tolerant metropolis as far as race was concerned in the 1890's, Cleveland provided a setting where Ransom's developing anti-Washington views received a positive response.

Even within church circles, questions concerning Washington's overall approach received a hearing. By 1897, the Iowa Annual Conference's Committee on Education, of which Ransom was secretary, while giving its qualified support to industrial education, stressed that the church's primary task had to be devoted to providing trained leaders for its people--leaders who

133

would lift their people intellectually, spiritually and socially. There are aspects within that report of DuBois' later concept of the "talented tenth."[14] While the Committee's criticism of industrial education as the sole pedagogical course for Blacks is implicitly stated in the Conference's proceedings, Ransom was very explicit about his misgivings concerning industrial education and Booker T. Washington. In an 1897 Indianapolis Freeman article, Ransom suggested that Washington had made the mistake of speaking out of his limited experience and wrote, "It seems to me that he would make the needs of his institution represent the needs of the race."[15] Ransom contended that Washington's position on the race question and its solution was most welcome to the majority of white citizens, since it conformed to their view about the position which Blacks should occupy within the society. Ransom recognized the great response Washington's philosophy received from white America and acknowledged his growing influence of power within black America. However, Ransom quesitoned whether white America's sincerity could be trusted and observed that many Blacks supported Washington for pecuniary and political gain by stating "There is now a regular swarm of little Booker T. Washingtons springing up all over the country."[16]

Washington's ascendancy to racial leadership, the sudden appearance of "little Booker T. Washingtons" and the shift from protest to accommodation among black organizations and institutions are clearly reflected in the history and development of the Afro-American League, later renamed the Afro-American Council (1890-1908). Founded by T. Thomas Fortune, the militant socialist and firebrand editor of the New York Age, the League began its exitence in the mold of the abolitionist protest tradition. The League numbered among its members, Bishop Henry McNeal Turner, Ida Wells Barnett, W.E.B. DuBois, and Reverdy C. Ransom. Despite its sporadic activity, the League came to be increasingly influenced by Washington during the decade of the nineties. Depleting most of its energy with factionalism between the Washington and Anti-Washington wings within the organization, by the 1890's, the League was organizationally exhausted. Failing to meet for two years or more, it was revived in 1898 as the Afro-American Council under the leadership of African Methodist Episcopal Zion Bishop Alexander Walters. The Council was an amalgam of the protest and accomodationist strategies of the day. One historian, Emma Lou Thornbough, suggests that the Council's history "was inextricably linked with the fight over (Booker T.) Washington as race leader."[17] The events surrounding the Council's national meeting held in Chicago during August of 1899 is an illustration of that leadership struggle.

In the editorial, "The Afro-American Council," The Chicago Inter-Ocean essayed the meaning of the confab for the "colored race" and expressed opinion on the direction the Council's leadership should follow:

> The object of their meeting is to improve the condition of the colored race. How to accomplish this end is a question that they answer in diverse ways. There are men like Bishop Turner who believe that race prejudice is so strong in this country that the only hope for the colored people is wholesale immigration. There are others who believe that education will solve the problem satisfactorily. We believe that the majority of intelligent men, outside of the Afro-American Council, will agree with the advocates of the education theory. All reports show that since the establishment of the Tuskegee Institute and other schools of the same character, great progress has been made in the South. Those engaged in this industrial and educational work do not lay great stress on the entrance of colored men into political life. Their aim is to strengthen character, educate the colored people to careers of usefulness, and to encourage the young people of their race to break away from old traditions, old customs, and work out their own salvation as young people among the Whites are expected to do...The significant thing in the above record is that the most improvement is due to efforts made by the colored people themselves.[18]

The Inter-Ocean reflected the concerned white opinion of the day and framed the deliberations of the Council as a plebiscite for or against the Washinton strategy. The Inter-Ocean was correct in its

135

assessment, since the radical and conservative forces within the Council battled each other most fiercely over the adoption of various resolutions during the meeting. W.E.B. DuBois and Reverdy C. Ransom were members of the resolution drafting committee, as was Washington's operative, T.T. Allain. Washington's supporters within the Council successfully squashed or diluted most of the radical pronouncements, including a proposed statement on lynching. Radicals, such as Ida B. Wells and Reverdy Ransom were defeated in their attempts to pass a strongly worded resolution condemning President McKinley for his silence on lynching. Washington's supporters feared that the defeated resolution, if it had passed, might have been preceived as a repudiation not only of Washington's close ties to the President, but of his own preeminent leadership within the American Negro community.[19] Despite the powerful lobbying efforts of Washington's forces, the Council did resolve, in the spirit of protest, to demand that the government protect black life, and condemned the practice of basing the right to vote on race and not on intelligence and property. Finally, it resolved that black people were American citizens despite the fact that they were denied their rights and privileges by the nation.[20] The radicals continued to hold key positions within the Council as Ida Wells Barnett was elected secretary and Ransom was chosen as eighth vice president.[21]

Although present in the city, Booker T. Washington did not attend the Council meeting, but sent his wife instead. He had been advised by T. Thomas Fortune to absent himself from the meeting lest some of the Council "hot heads"[22] embarrass him by passing inflammatory resolutions. Although he did not appear on the convention floor, Washington caucused in his hotel room with Council President Alexander Walters and other supporters. Washington's absence from the Council sessions emboldened a small group of radicals, led by Reverdy C. Ransom, to offer a resolution condemning Washington for refusing to attend the meeting and for Mrs. Washington's last minute withdrawal from the program. Ransom also tried unsuccessfully to have Washington's name stricken from the Council's membership list as well.

Although they perceived the unsuccessful attacks as the endeavors of "little hypocritical fellows,"[23] Washington and his followers were quick to respond to them by drafting and sending to friendly newspapers across the country disclaimers that Washington's leadership had been challenged. They also called upon their friends and allies within the Council and throughout the national black community to rise to Washington's defense and to condemn his attackers.[24] The response was swift and thunderous.

Reacting to a barrage of criticism following the incident, Ransom attempted to justify his actions by saying,

> ...I regarded it as unfortunate that we could not have present with us Booker T. Washington, as he was in the city, and generally regarded by the nation as the leading Negro of the race. I said that Mr. Washington, the educator, was right in staying away from the convention if he thought it was likely to commit itself by some intemperate speech, which, if he was associated with it, might injure his school; but it was the duty of Booker T. Washington, as the leader of his race, if he felt that we might go wrong, to come and set us right. I strongly protested against his manifest inclination to keep away from the convention, because of his exalted position as a recognized leader of his race.[25]

Because of Washington's "exalted position" and the brashness of their actions, Ransom and his accomplices were unaimously repudiated and disavowed when the Council expressed its continued admiration and appreciation of Washington's leadership, and its president, Alexander Walers, defended the integrity of his motives. Even W.E.B. DuBois considered Ransom's words "ill-timed and foolish."[26] Referring to the Council meeting, DuBois said,

> The spirit of the gathering was not represented at all in the remarks of Mr. Ransom, and I deeply regret that anything of the kind took place. Nearly everyone in the convention is also of my opinion, and I should be very sorry if it went out to the world that this convention had said anything

detrimental to one of the greatest men
of our race.[27]

Under the weight of such criticism, Ransom wrote
Washington, denying that he had spoken of him
disrespectfully or that he had sought "to misrepresent
or do you harm."[28] What he had wanted to convey was his
conviction that Washington should have been present to
share his wisdom and experience as the Council
deliberated upon the social, industrial, educational,
financial and civil conditions of the race. Ransom
wrote to Washington apologizing for any damage his words
might have caused and said, "I regard your career as one
of the most fruitful and remarkable of any man of our
race..."[29] However, such glowing sentiments could not
conceal Ransom's wariness of Washington's approach to
racial uplift. In an article published in the A.M.E.
Review a few months after his letter to Washington,
Ransom criticized the Tuskeegan's strategy by noting

>...that Mr. Washington and his associates
>hope to lift their race through preparing
>them for individual opportunities, by
>thrift, education and the moral and
>religious forces. Nothing is said about
>politics, no reference is made to politi-
>cal action, which has been thought so long
>by many to be the lever by which the race
>would be lifted to the enjoyment of its
>right.[30]

While Washington publicly eschewed involvement for
Blacks within American politics, he commanded a very
forceful and well-formed private polical machine which
had by 1902 captured control of the Afro-American
Council. This control by Washington's men was so
obvious that a group of radicals from New England, led
by the Bostonian, Monroe Trotter, unsucessfully
attempted to challenge their domination and power during
the Council's 1903 convention held in Louisville,
Kentucky.[31] Trotter and George Forbes, editors of the
Boston Guardian, were among the earliest and most
persistently severe critics of Washington's philosophy.
Following the Louisville meeting, an incident involving
Trotter, Forbes and Booker T. Washington did much to
widen the breach between the radical and conservative
groups.

Addressing a public meeting held in Boston in 1903, Washington was heckled and interrupted from the audience by questions from Trotter, Forbes and others. The disturbers were arrested and Trotter served a short jail term. The incident, dubbed "The Boston Riot,"[32] became for many of Washington's critics the most blatant example of his "political dictatorship"[33] and his imperial power. According to the radical newspaper, The Washington Bee,

> Booker T. Washington has become such an autocrat lately that he absolutely refused to answer the questions which are of vital importance to the Negro... White men may support him, but they can never ram him down the throats of the Afro-Americans as their new Moses, for he believes in building up his own popularity by walking over the dead bodies of his black brothers.[34]

"The Boston Riot" also caused some members of the white press to acknowledge the possibility that Washington's position was not the sole view held by black people. The Literary Digest, in an article, "The Opposition to Booker T. Washington," reported that opposition to Washington had developed among some Blacks and that its growth consisted of editorial statements and individual comments supporting or rejecting the contention that the majority of Blacks supported the Tuskegee educator. Quoting from a sermon delivered by Ransom at the Institutional Church in Chicago, the Digest indicated that he disagreed with those who suggested that Washington's leadership was overwhelmingly supported by Blacks. Ransom said, on the contrary, there were many who opposed "the surrender of our rights...(and) there would be others if Mr. Washington did not control the strong papers conducted by colored men and if they (the papers) expressed the sentiments of the people."[35]

W.E.B. Dubois, who had sought to occupy the middle ground between the Trotter and Washington camps, incurred the wrath of the Tuskegee machine when he published a statement in the Boston Guardian charging that several black newspapers had "sold out" to Washington. For DuBois, however, the Boston Riot was the event which cemented his outright opposition to Booker T. Washington. DuBois recalled that "...when Trotter went to jail, my indignation overflowed and...I proposed a conference during the summer "to oppose firmly present methods of stangling honest criticism; to organize intelligent and honest Negroes; and to support organs of news and public opinion."[36]

Richard R. Wright remembered the formation of the Niagara Movement in a different manner. Wright, who served as Ransom's assistant at the Institutional Church in Chicago, recalled that the Men's Club of the church read and discussed DuBois' Souls of Black Folk sometime after its publication in 1903. According to Wright, Ransom suggested that the club invite DuBois to Chicago to lead a three-day session on the "Negro American's position in America." The attendance at the meetings were small, but at its conclusion, a committee chosen by DuBois met at the residence of Chicago dentist, Charles E. Bentley and planned to call a meeting of prominent Blacks in order to establish a national organization committed to the struggle for manhood rights.[37]

With the Afro-American Council under the control of Booker T. Washington, an organization to counter the conservatives was desparately necessary, Wright recalled. The call to organize was sent to fifty-nine men and twenty-nine from fourteen states attended the founding session at Niagara Falls. Dr. Charles Bentley represented the Chicago area. Although Ransom was not present at the first meeting, he was an active Niagarite, serving on its Committee on Civil Rights and as a member of the Planning Committee for its Third Annual Meeting held in Boston in 1907.[38] (Ransom pastored Charles Street A.M.E. Church in the anti-Washington stronghold of Boston from 1904 to 1907). Becuase of his oratorical skill, Ransom was chosen to deliver addresses at the 1906 and 1907 Niagara meetings. His oration on John Brown, delivered on August 17, 1906 at Harpers Ferry, Virginia, was considered by J. Max Barber, the editor of the militant journal, the Voice of the Negro "(as) the most eloquent address this writer has ever listened to. He spoke of the spirit of John Brown, and before he was through speaking, everbody in the house must have felt that John Brown's spirit was with us...Women wept, men shouted and waved hats and handkerchiefs, and everybody was moved," Barber recounted.[39] DuBois was no less effusive in his praise of Ransom's Harpers Ferry address when he recalled that "...(the) speech, more than any single event, stirred the great meeting."[40]

In his tribute to John Brown, Ransom described the characteristic approaches of the conservative and radical groups as he understood them:

> One counsels patient submission to our present humiliations and degradations; it deprecates political activity, ignores or condones the unsurpation and denial of our politcial and constitutional rights and preaches the doctrine of property, while it has not word of protest or condemnation for those who visit upon us all manner of fiendish and human indignities...The other class believes that it should not submit to inferior place...It does not believe that those who toil and accumulate will be free to enjoy the fruts of their industry and frugality, if they permit themselves to be shorn of political power...It believes that the Negro should assert his full title to American manhood, and maintain every right guaranteed him by the Constitution of the United States.[41]

Ransom expressed similar insights in an address delivered in Boston a year earlier:

> There are two views of the Negro question. One is that the Negro should stoop to conquer; that he should accept in silence the denial of his political rights; that he should not brave the displeasure of white men by protesting when he is segregated in humilating ways...There are others who believe that the Negro owes this nation no apoplogy for his presence...; that being black, he is still no less a man; that he should refuse to be assigned to an inferior place by his fellow countrymen.[42]

Despite the brave rhetoric of Ransom and the aggressive posture of DuBois, Trotter, and other Niagarites, the movement floundered almost from the beginning. Its program for racial equality was far ahead of its time, advocating as it did freedom of speech, the right to vote, the ending of discrimination based on race in public accommodations, equal justice

141

for the poor as well as the rich and equal justice for Blacks as well as Whites, the right to employment, and the right to have black children educated "as intelleigent human beings...(and not) simply as servants and underlings."43 The Niagara Movement's weakness was also exacerbated by the power and strength of the Tuskegee machine, the radicals' inability to relate to the black masses, and, as Ransom later recalled, the personal conflicts and disagreement between Monroe Trotter and W.E.B. DuBois.44 Although relatively short-lived and essentially ineffective in its thrust, the Niagara Movement, by alerting sympathic Whites to its militant posture, became the forerunner of the interracial NAACP. Prior to the founding of the NAACP, however, Ransom was a member of another short-lived interracial organization, the Constitution League headed by manufacturer, John Milholland. Milholland, a progressive Republican, engaged in numerous reform movements, founded the League, "...to attack disfranchisement, peonage, and racial violence by means of court action, legislation and propaganda."45 The League's members included, besides Ransom, Alexander Walters, Monroe Trotter and J. Max Barber.46 Another white progressive, Oswald Garrison Villard, grandson of William Lloyd Garrison, was so outraged by the race riot in Springfield, Illinois in 1908 that he and a few other Whites, William English Walling, Dr. Henry Moskowitz and Mary White Ovington, called a National Conference on the Negro Quesiton for New York City, February 12, 1909. Pastoring Bethel A.M.E. Church in New York at the time, Ransom was one of the persons invited to attend that meeting.

The formal organizational structure of the NAACP was developed at the second conference the following year, and Ransom, along with the majority of the Niagarites and Constitution League members (with the exception of Trotter and Ida B. Wells) joined with white progressives such as long-time Ransom associates, Clarence Darrow and Jane Addams to form the new protest organization.47

In an address delivered to the NAACP's founding meeting in 1910 entitled "Democracy, Disfranchisement and the Negro," Ransom forcefully articulated the radicals' unswerving commitment to acquiring the right to vote and their determination to agitate and protest until those rights were assured. Despite the hopes of President Taft, the Congress and the Supreme Court that

142

protest would cease, Ransom warned the gathering that until the question of disfranchisement was addressed, agitation would continue:

> This quesiton is far too vital to the very existence of our democracy to be hushed up, ignored, compromised, abandoned or surrendered. It will continue to disturb, to agitate, and imperil the nation, ramifying into every phase of its industrial, social and political life, until settled.[48]

Black people were as much Americans as any other group, he asseted, and deserved to be accorded their full citizenship rights. The mark of a free man was his right to vote, and Ransom urged immediate action. The black man, he insisted, "...will not only demand the right to vote and be voted for, but he will refuse to be debarred from the privilege of assisting in framing and administering the laws under which he lives."[49]

Ransom's courageous words were more easily said then done. Not only was southern black disfranchisement nearly complete in 1910, but the Republican Party, to whom Blacks had given their loyalty since Recontruction, had acquiesced in that disfranchisement. Black leaders like Ransom had to fight for the right to vote, while endeavoring to align themselves with a political party that would be responsive to their people's needs and not use their votes, as had the GOP over the years, for its own benefit. Political scientist Charles V. Hamilton writes,

> This has been a dilemma throughout the black political experience: on the one hand, to advocate political involvement in institutions deliberately designed to disappoint and therefore lead possibly to alienation and withdrawal on the part of Blacks; on the other hand to counsel non-participation and non-cooperation with no acceptable alternative, and therefore lead possibly to a vacuum and alienation. From Reconstruction on, this has been he unenviable role of black leaders; i.e., to chart a course that avoids these results and at the same time to engage in political action

143

calculated to bring about some meaningful benefits.[50]

Reverdy Ransom's political involvements between
1890 and 1932 are most clearly understood in light of
the limited options available to Blacks during those
years.

Voting rights for Blacks had been a major
consideration of a victorious Republican Party following
the Civil War. Through its efforts, the Fifteenth
Amendment was passed and the G.O.P. gained virtual sway
over the black vote for more than half a century. The
black vote in the North was no less locked into the
Republican fold. The Ohio of Ransom's youth and young
adulthood was a powerful center of black Republicans. A
number of Ransom's professional and social colleagues,
such as Jere A. Brown, John P. Green and Cleveland
Gazette editor, Harry C. Smith were elected to the State
Legislature as Republicans. George A. Myers, the barber
businessman, was a trusted confidante and political
adviser to Ohio Republican boss, Mark Hanna, as was
Ransom's friend, Bishop Benjamin Arnett.[51] It was
through such contacts that Ransom was invited to address
the Sixth Annual Lincoln Banquet in Columbus, Ohio on
February 14, 1893. In the speech entitled "The
Fifteenth Amendment," he called upon the Republican
Party to reject the overtures of the white South as it
sought to woo the party away from its commitment to
black political and civil rights. Ransom urged the
banquet audience to remember that the Negro had been
loyal and grateful even as his party appointed him to
small offices, "with the promise of better things to
come."[52] Likening Blacks to a faithful and satisfied
old woman, Ransom reminded the gathering that "the Negro
is Republican in season and out of season."[53]

Even while avowing black loyalty and devotion to
the Republican Party in an attempt to prod the Party's
conscience, Ransom noted the silence of the Republican
press and prominent Republican leaders to the
disfranchisement of southern Blacks. Blacks were being
abandoned because the Republican Party complained that
it lacked the governmental power to prevent the states
from enacting disfranchising legislation. Ransom
doubted if such powerlessness would avail if Blacks were
disfranchising Whites. He wrote,

But it is my deliberate judgment and

144

solemn belief that if Negroes were
surrounding the ballot boxes with
shot guns and keeping white men from
the polls, we would find a way to
stop it. If Negroes were fraudently
seizing the representation in score
of congressional districts and the
electoral vote in a dozen states, we
would find a way to stop it.[54]

At the time, Ohio's black Republican leadership
endeavored to enhance its postion within the national
Republican Party. Although certain factions, led by
George A. Myers, Benjamin Arnett and Harry C. Smith,
sought preeminence, all camps were frustrated by the
strong influence that their black southern brethren, led
by Booker T. Washington, had on Mark Hanna. This was
the case primarily because the black population in the
1890's was located overwhelmingly in the South.
Controlling as it did the northern and southern black
vote, the party, through Hanna, meted out political
appointments based upon its assessment of the power of
each section. Still, the election of 1896 afforded
northern Blacks, and especially black Ohioans, the
opportunity to show their political mettle and their
ability to support the national ticket. Ohio Governor
William McKinley became the Republican Party
standard-bearer in the election. His presidential
campaign was run by Mark Hanna, who established the
National Republican Headquarters in Chicago. The
Afro-American Bureau, a branch of the Republican
National Committee, was officed in the National
Headquarters building. Ransom was pastoring Bethel
A.M.E. Church in Chicago at the time and remembered
meeting Robert Lincoln, President Lincoln's son and
Theodore Roosevelt at the National Headquarters
building.[55] The Bureau, headed by Ferdinand L. Barnett,
the husband of Ransom's parishoner and friend, Ida B.
Wells, coordinated black Republican activities in
various states for the McKinley campaign. Assisted by a
board of executive committeemen in the states, the
Bureau was enormously successful in consolidating black
votes for the Republican presidential nominee. The
Bureau used the black press to get out the vote and
enlisted, through a Speakers Bureau, prominent Blacks to
speak on McKinley's behalf throughout the country. Over
150 such rallies were held in Ohio alone, and Blacks
nationally cast over 400,000 votes for McKinley and his
running-mate.[56]

With the election of McKinley, the competition for
political prestige and influence between George A. Myers
and Harry C. Smith became intense. Both men and their
partisans advanced the idea that each was more influential with Mark Hanna than the other. Both groups sought
to curry political favor with Hanna and lobbied for
political appointments for their allies. While Ransom
did not seek political position, he was a strong
supporter of Myers. It is possible that Ransom's
defense of Myers was more personal than political.
Myers had been an active member of Cleveland's St.
John's A.M.E. Church when Ransom pastored there and may
have provided Ransom with the necessary funds to cover
some unnamed difficulty.[57] It appears that Ransom was
grateful for Myers' kindness. Whatever the reason,
Ransom waged a campaign against Harry C. Smith's
allegations that the only influence Myers had with Hanna
was as a "lackey and valet." Ransom countered by saying
that Hanna has called upon Myers, not as a valet or
lackey, but as a trusted political lieutenant. The
controversy continued for a number of months.[58]

Despite his spirited defense of Myers and his
friendship with other patronange seekers such as John P.
Green, Claude A. Barnett, and Benjamin Arnett, Ransom
was not primarily concerned about the political feuding
of his associates or their efforts to divide paltry
political spoils. He was vitally interested in issues
affecting Blacks, such as the new President's position
on lynching, black disfranchisement, and the Chief
Executive's thoughts about future nominees to the
Suprememe Court. He wrote,

> ...There are matters of such great moment
> to every vital interest of the race that
> they should not be neglected. Those
> recognized as leaders by the press and
> others should seek to influence policy
> along the lines of vital interest to the
> race. This is far more important than
> dividing spoils.[59]

Lynching and politcal disfranchisement were uppermost in
Ransom's mind, and he believed that McKinley was
consitutionally obligated to use the power of the
Federal Government to protect black lives and their
right to vote.

McKinley revealed the essence of his racial policy

during his inaugural address when he promised to "do nothing to disturb the growing sentiment of unity and cooperation" between the North and South. Like Rutherford B. Hayes before him, McKinley promised not to jeopardize the developing cordial relations between the two sections. Ransom denounced McKinley's stance as courting the lily-white South, even though John P. Green, George A. Myers, and Benjamin Arnett cautioned calm and patience, and Harry C. Smith labeled Ransom's criticism as ridiculous and ill-founded.

President McKinley also remained silent as southern lynchings escalated and successful efforts to deny black suffrage continued. Ransom attacked McKinley's callous disregard of the constitutionally guaranteed rights of black citizens and their right to protection from lawless white mobs. President McKinley continued his silence in 1898 when a white mob in Wilmington, North Carolina killed many Blacks. While Benjamin Arnett and John P. Green counselled McKinley's silence, Ransom warned that if such mob attacks continued, Blacks would be driven to arm themselves. Ransom concluded that the G.O.P. had betrayed the loyalty and trust of black people and no longer deserved their support.60

The dilemma facing Ransom and other radicals during the late 1890's and the years following it was the absence of a political party to which to go. Thus, even while the Republicans treated them with little respect by taking their votes for granted, Blacks could not switch to the Democrats, who openly condoned and oft-times advocated white violence against them, particularly in the South. Thus, neither political party was interested in protecting the political or legal rights of Blacks. The old black spiritual was right. "There was no hiding (political) place down here."61 Thus, by 1899, Ransom and other radicals within the Afro-American Council adopted a resolution favoring a new politcal party and pledged themselves to oppose those who failed to support protection for black voters. However, these northern radicals lacked the resources to heal divisions in the black community and lacked the clout and numbers to form new political structures. Since the majority of Blacks lived in the South, their dwindling electoral vote, disclaimed by the lily-white Democrats, was locked into the Republican fold. Northern black Republican leaders, on the other hand, were engaged in their own internal struggles for political influence and partonage within the national party.

Booker T. Washington became the "political broker" of Roosevelt and Taft in the dispensing of political appointment and patronage positions to Blacks around the country. Both presidents endeavored through Washington to assure the order and stability party discipline required. No analysis of the long and bitter conflict between the radicals and the conservatives can be undertaken without examining that struggle in light of the political situations of the times.

Radicals such as Trotter generally disdained and mistrusted black politicians, recognizing as he did the politicians' dependence on Booker T. Washington for their positions. Most radicals believed that it was necessary for Blacks to free themselves from absolute allegiance to the Republican Party. It was time, they said, for Blacks to cast their ballots on the basis of the candidate's commitment to black concerns rather than his party affiliation. Even so, Blacks had few available political choices. The Presidential election of 1904 is a case in point. Because the Democratic candidate, Alton B. Parker, was even more objectionable than Theodore Roosevelt, the Republican candidate, Trotter and other radicals urged Blacks to vote for the G.O.P. standard-bearer. The radicals were forced to support Roosevelt even though they were aware that their interests did not rank high on his political agenda.[62]

In 1901, Roosevelt immediately set out to wrest control of the party apparatus from Ohio's Senator Mark Hanna after the assassination of William McKinley. Hanna's ability to control national conventions was due to his influence among mid-western and southern delegates. He had guided McKinley to the presidency and used executive power to appoint lily-white Republicans to Federal offices in the South. National convention delegates were invariably chosen from those office-holders. In order to combat Hanna's lily-white Republican organization in the South, Roosevelt maneuvered to resurrect in that section the "Old Black and Tan" coalition of early Reconstruction years. In order to recruit people loyal to him, Roosevelt needed, among others, the kind of black southern leader to advise him on political matters who was discreet, accommodating, and who avoided conflict with his white southern neighbors. Booker T. Washington was the ideal choice. Thus, Roosevelt's White House dinner meeting

148

with Washington in 1901, despite accusations by much of white America that it signalled Roosevelt's advocacy of social equality among the races, was much more political than social in its intent. Both Roosevelt and Washington were pleased at the arrangement agreed upon at the dinner. The President was able to select federal officials in the South favorable to his administration and thereby, with Washington's assistance, guarantee his control of the Republican Party. While in like manner, the Tuskegee educator, with the prestige accompanying his role as Presidential advisor, increased his control of the national black community.[63]

By the 1904 Presidential election Roosevelt had not only successfully maintained the "Black and Tan" coalition, but had also won the support of a sizeable proportion of Hanna's lily-white Republicans. Sensing that reconciliation with the white southern wing of the party was imminent, thereby assuring absolute party control, Roosevelt began to speak favorably of the southern way of life (i.e., its policies having to do with Blacks). Following Washington's lead, he also urged Blacks to ignore higher studies for industrial education.

While these statements by Roosevelt aroused the ire of the radicals, no event galvanized their opposition to him more than his actions following "the Brownsville Incident" in 1906. Following a riot alledgedly led by black soldiers in that Texas town, Roosevelt immediately discharged three companies of the 25th army regiment. By dismissing the soldiers without the benefit of a hearing or a trial, Roosevelt seemed to impugn the character and integrity of American Blacks. Blacks across the country were unanimous in their anger against the President. Even Washington's loyalists were appalled.[64] Reverdy Ransom, along with Monroe Trotter and other radicals, participated in a protest meeting at Fancuil Hall in Boston. Both signed a statement deploring the discharges as "unmerited severity, unprecedented injustice and wanton abuse of executive power..."[65] By the 1908 Presidential election, a significant number of radicals, having grown increasingly disillusioned with Roosevelt and the Republican Party, gave their support to William Jennings Bryan, the Democratic canididate. Led by Trotter and African Methodist Episcopal Zion Bishop Alexander Walters, they organized the National Negro American Political League.[66] Booker T. Washington supported the victorious Republican candidate, William Howard Taft. Washington continued in his role as political broker with Taft as he had with Roosevelt. Since Taft had been Secretary of War during Brownsville, many Blacks were wary of him. The new administration began inauspiciously as far as Blacks were concerned, when Taft promised to appoint no federal officials opposed by the South.

Ransom considered Taft's statement "insulting" to black people, and particularly demeaning in the face of black people's "slavish devotion to the Republican Party..."[67] He counselled Blacks to vote for individuals and not parties, and suggested uniting with the Socialist Party if necessary.[68]

It is doubtful that the pragmatic Ransom seriously considered the Socialist Party as a real option for black voters. It is not unlikely that he agreed with DuBois, a Socialist at the time, that Blacks would be throwing away their votes by supporting the Socialist ticket. DuBois resigned his membership in the Socialist Party prior to the Presidential election of 1912.[69] Radicals were convinced that the political realities of that election required Blacks to courageously break with their political tradition and consider other options. The election of 1912 epitomized the risks involved for Blacks when other political alternatives were tried.

Three major candidates sought the presidency in 1912; the Republican incumbent, Taft; his Democratic challenger, Woodrow Wilson; and the third party candidate of the Bull Moose or Progressive Party, Theodore Roosevelt. Most radicals, being thoroughly disenchanted with Taft and wary of Wilson the southerner, supported Roosevelt, with varying degrees of enthusiasm. DuBois hoped that Roosevelt's new party would support "...a broad platform of votes for Negroes and the decentralization of industry."[70] Ransom supported Roosevelt's candidacy as well. However, both Ransom and DuBois withdrew their support from Theodore Roosevelt when the candidate refused to seat black delegates from the South during the Progressive Party convention, but welcomed the lily-white delegates instead.[71]

DuBois joined African Methodist Episcopal Zion Bishop Alexander Walters, President of the National Colored Democratic League, and Monroe Trotter, and

supported the Democratic candidate, Woodrow
Wilson,[72] while Booker T. Washington supported Taft. It
is not altogether clear whom Ransom supported after his
disavowal of Roosevelt. It appears that he remained
uncommitted; however, it is clear that as editor of the
A.M.E. Review, he provided black Democratic and
Republican spokesman opportunity to defend their
candidates in the pages of the Review. The October 1912
volume of the Review featured an article favoring Wilson
by James S. Curtis, Chairman of the Campaign Committee
and Secretary of the National Colored Democratic
Organization's Executive Committee, and Washington's
confidante, Fred R. Moore, editor of the New York Age,
who urged Taft's election.[73] Ransom did not seem
enthusiastic about any of the candidates, although he
was excited about the opportunity that Blacks possessed
to break their absolute allegiance to the Republican
Party. His optimism for the future involved the
emergence of what he described as a "new political
consciousness" among Blacks.[74]

The outcome of the 1912 election and the way in
which Blacks cast their ballots during the contest
seemed sweet portents of that new political awareness.
Most Blacks voted for Roosevelt, while the remainder
evenly divided their votes between Taft and Wilson.
Kelly Miller saw the balloting as a sign of the
"political emancipation" of black people and Ransom
exulted that for once, "...the Negro cannot be safely
counted en masse as the political property of any
party."[75] Bishop Walters expressed the underlying
strategy of the radicals when he said, "...With a
division of the black vote, we will have political
friends in both parties."[76]

Since the President-elect, during his campaign, had
appealed for and received black support by promising to
be just in his approach to their concerns, radicals such
as Walters, Trotter, DuBois and Ransom trusted Wilson to
keep his word. Walters expressed that trust in an
article written for the A.M.E. Review when he wrote:

> The election of Woodrow Wilson means a
> dawn of a new era to the Negroes of this
> country...I believe it will be the aim
> of Governor Wilson to give to the Negroes
> of the South a political status such as
> they have not had in recent years...It is
> my opinion that he will breathe into the

151

Amendments (the thirteenth, fourteenth
and fifteenth) the breath of life, and
give to the Constitution as far as the
Negro is concerned, a living soul.[77]

Walter's optimism could not have been more
ill-founded. Under Woodrow Wilson, the segregated
practices within federal departments, begun by Taft,
became the rule rather than the exception. Wilson's key
advisors were firm believers in segregation, as was his
entire cabinet. Blacks were segregated in most
governmental departments, including the Bureau of the
Census, the Bureau of Printing and Engraving and the
Post Office. Segregation practices began to quietly
pervade the entire apparatus of the government as
offices, shops, rest-rooms and restaurants in
Washington, D.C. became Jim Crowed.[78] Voting rights in
the South were either ignored or crushed under Wilson,
resulting in the total disfranchisement of Blacks. The
triumph of the lily-white South was complete. Alexander
Walters expressed the rising protest and anger of Blacks
who had trustingly supported Wilson when he wrote,

I regret to say that (Wilson) has failed to
realize any of the expectations by his fair
promises and sweet-sounding phrases about
justice and equal opportunity uttered in
pre-election days. His "New Freedom," it
seems, has been all for the white man and
little for the Negro.[79]

Ransom accused Wilson and his administration's advocacy
of racial segregation as being "unpatriotic,
undemocratic, and fiendish."[80] When a delegation of
black Democrats, led by Monroe Trotter, met with the
President and expressed their feelings of betrayal at
his segregationist policies, Wilson accused Trotter of
insolence and bad manners. Ransom defended Trotter and
lauded his Boston friend's courage, integrity and
commitment to racial justice and equality.[81]

Ransom later recalled that it was Wilson, not
Trotter, who had been insulting to black people by
breaking his "solemn" promise to give them justice. "He
broke all promises, (and) permitted (the) segregation of
government employees, (taking) no active measures to
stop lynching and beating, (and) did not rebuke
disfranchisement," Ransom wrote.[82]

The radical soon realized that their efforts to broaden their people's political viability were to be destroyed by the racist policies of the Democratic Party. DuBois wrote,

> We had calculated that increased indepen-
> dence in the Negro vote would bring a bid
> for the Negro vote from opposing parties;
> but it did not until many years later.
> Indeed, it was not until the re-election
> of the second Roosevelt in 1936 that the
> Negro vote in the North came to be eagerly
> contended for by the two major parties.83

Thus by 1916, DuBois continued, "We found ourselves politically helpless. We had no choice. We could not vote for Wilson who had segregated us or for (Charles Evans) Hughes who, despite all our requests, remained doggedly dumb on our problems."84 Despite Hughes' lack of concern, most Blacks, including Ransom, having no alternative, supported his losing presidential candidacy. However, Ransom analyzed the defeat philosophically. "The Republican Party does not deserve to win until it is chastened in spirit and firmly resolved to take its stand for political justice."85 Ransom's anger at the Republican Party was exacerbated by what he considered its long history of black betrayal, neglect, and unfaithfulness to racial justice.

Despite Ransom's belief that the Republicans were not deserving of its support, the black community had no other political alternative after 1912 but to drift back to the Party of Lincoln. Ransom's political odyssey from 1916 to 1932 is indicative of his struggle to find a way out of the political quagmire. He ran as an independent candidate for Congress from New York's Twenty-First Congressional District (which included Harlem) in 1918 after the Republican organiztion refused to nominate him. The organization went to court and successfully prevented his name from appearing on the ballot. Nevertheless, 465 persons voted for him as a write in candidate.

Ransom was urged to run by the black businessman realtor John M. Royall and was supported by Royall's United Civic League. Although Ransom failed to win, he also prevented the Republican candidate from winning, since a large number of Blacks boycotted the

election.[86] This losing Congressional campaign was
initiated by Ransom and the United Civic League to
arouse and encourage black voters to demand recognition
in New York and in other northern cities and to warn the
New York Republican Organiation that they could not
expect to win elections if they ignored black voters.[87]

During the 1920 Presidential race, Ransom supported
Republican Warren Harding against his Democratic
opponent, John W. Davis, citing the G.O.P. as the lesser
of two evils. He sought to rationalize that support by
urging Blacks to agitate for and fight to change the
party's racial stance from within.[88] Although Ransom
reluctantly supported the Republican candidacy of Calvin
Coolidge in 1924, by 1928 he was openly supporting the
Democratic Presidential candidacy of Governor Al Smith
of New York. Although he found that Blacks had been
ignored by the Democratic Party, Ransom witnessed years
of exploitation of Blacks by Republicans and therefore
he chose to align himself with Smith. Ransom joined the
Smith-for-President Colored League and chaired the
organization's Speakers Bureau.[89] Writing in the
November 1932 issue of _Crisis_, Ransom appealed to Blacks
to vote for the Democratice Presidential candidate,
Franklin D. Roosevelt. Hoover, he said, had never
supported loyal black southern Republicans, but the
lily-white Republicans instead.[90] During the
Congressional elections in 1934, Ransom echoed the hopes
and sentiments of Alexander Walters twenty-two years
earlier when he said, "Although Negroes have blindly
followed the Republican ticket, their party has betrayed
and abandoned them. The Negroes should, therefore, make
friends with former foes and seek, by giving them
political support, to win a larger measure of
justice."[91]

With the 1934 Congressional election and the
Presidential election of 1936, Blacks severed their
historic allegiance to the Republican Party. Reverdy C.
Ransom led the way to what became ironically, yet
another historic allegiance in that instance to the
Democratic rather than the Republican Party. That this
was not Ransom's aim is clearly revealed in an address
he delivered on November 3, 1934 entitled "The Negroes'
Bewildering Political Predicament:"

We do not need to vote the entire Republican ticket or the entire Democratic ticket,
but (for) the men on each ticket who offer

154

us political recognition, political hope
and political advancement...Above all, let
us cease to be the political slaves and
retainers of any political party.[92]

Despite Ransom's hope and many years of struggle, he
helped lead Blacks out of one political bondage and
into another.

Footnotes

[1]Ransom, <u>The Spirit of Freedom and Justice</u>, p. 75.

[2]Kenneth M. Stampp, <u>The Era of Reconstruction—1865-1877</u> (New York: Vantage Books, 1965), pp. 186-215.

[3]C. Vann Woodward, <u>Origins of the New South, 1877-1913</u> (Baton Rouge: Louisiana State University Press, 1951), pp. 321-39.

[4]Howard University Dean and Professor Kelly Miller used the term in an essay of the same name, "Radicals and Conservatives" in his book <u>Race Adjustment</u>, written in 1908. The work was republished 60 years later as <u>Radicals and Conservatives and Other Essays on the Negro in America</u> (New York: Schocken Books, 1968); <u>Booker T. Washington" The Making of a Black Leader</u> (New York: Oxford University Press, 1972), p. 260.

[5]Ransom, <u>Spirit of Freedom and Justice</u>, p. 111. For additional information regarding the "two contending camps," see James Weldon Johnson, <u>Black Manhattan</u> (1930 rpt., New York: Atheneum Press, 1969), p. 134; <u>Along This Way</u> (1933 rpt., New York: Viking Press, 1968), p. 313.

[6]Miller, <u>Radicals and Conservatives</u>, pp. 25-26.

[7]Emmett Jay Scott, Washington's private secretary, called his boss the "Wizard." See Louis R. Harlan, <u>Booker T. Washington: The Making of a Black Leader</u> (New York: Oxford University Press, 1972), p. 260.

[8]See Harlan, <u>Booker T. Washington: The Making of a Black Leader, 1856-1901</u>, pp. 204-71 for an excellent discussion of Washington's power and influence.

[9]Ransom, <u>Pilgrimage</u>, p. 163.

[10]Meier, <u>Negro Thought in America</u>, pp. 100-08; Woodward, <u>Origin of the New South</u>, pp. 356-60.

[11]For the classic statement defining the opposition, see W.E.B. DuBois' essay, "On Mr. Booker T. Washington and Others,: <u>The Souls of Black Folk</u> (1903; rpt. Chicago: Discos Books, 1968), pp. 240-52.

[12]Meier, <u>Negro Thought</u>, pp. 180, 221.

[13]Russell H. Davis, Black Americans in Cleveland (Washington, D.C.: The Associated Publishers, 1972), pp. 130-32.

[14]Minutes of the Fifteenth Annual Session, Iowa Annual Conference, 1897, pp. 33-35.

[15]Minutes of the Fifteenth Annual Session, Iowa Annual Conference; Reverdy C. Ransom, Indianapolis Freeman, March 20, 1897.

[16]Ransom, Indianapolis Freeman, March 20, 1897.

[17]Emma Lou Thornbough, "The Afro-American League, 1887-1908," Journal of Southern History 27, February 1961, quoted in Seth Scheiner's Negro Mecca, pp. 198-200, August Meier and Elliott M. Rudwick, From Plantation to Ghetto (New York: Hill and Wang, 1966), p. 182.

[18]Inter-Ocean, August 19, 1899, p. 6.

[19]Inter-Ocean, August 19, 1899, p. 5.

[20]Chicago Journal, August 19, 1899, n.p.

[21]Inter-Ocean, August 20, 1899, p. 5.

[22]Louis R. Harlan and Raymond W. Smock, eds., The Booker T. Washington Papers, 1899-1900 (Chicago: University of Chicago Press, 1976), p. 105.

[23]Harlan & Smock, The Booker T. Washington Papers, p. 181.

[24]Harlan, Booker T. Washington: The Making of a Black Leader, 1856-1901, pp. 262-64; Harlan and Smock, Washington Papers, pp. 186-87.

[25]Ransom, "Chicago Honored by the Race," The Christian Recorder, September 7, 1899, pp. 1, 6.

[26]Inter-Ocean, August 20, 1899, pp. 5-6.

[27]Inter-Ocean, August 20, 1899, pp. 5-6; Chicago Tribune, August 20, 1899; Harlan and Smock, Washington Papers 5, pp. 175-81.

[28]Harlan and Smock, The Washington Papers 5, p.

194.

[29]Harlan and Smock, Washington Papers 5, pp. 194-95.

[30]Reverdy C. Ransom "A Programme for the Negro," A.M.E. Review (April 1900).

[31]Stephen R. Fox, The Guardian of Boston, Monroe Trotter (New York: Atheneum, 1970), p. 46; Meier & Rudwick, From Plantation to Ghetto, pp. 182-83; Ransom, "Editorial, The Negro Sanhedrin," A.M.E. Review, April 1924, p. 214.

[32]Fox, The Guardian of Boston, p. 52.

[33]The Washington Bee, August 8, 1903, p. 4.

[34]Daniels, In Freedom's Birthplace, pp. 260-61; Fox, The Guardian of Boston, pp. 41, 53-54; The Washington Bee, August 8, 1903, p. 4; Ransom, Pilgrimage, pp. 153-62.

[35]"The Opposition to Booker T. Washington," The Literary Digest, 27, No. 7, August 15, 1903, pp. 188-89; Fox, The Guardian of Boston, p. 53.

[36]W.E.B. DuBois, Dusk of Dawn (1940 rpt., New York: Schocken Books, 1970), pp. 86-88; Ransom, Pilgrimage, pp. 161-62. DuBois mistakenly remembered the Boston Riot occurring in 1905 rather than in 1903.

[37]R. R. Wright, Eighty-Seven Years Behind the Black Curtain (Nashville: A.M.E. Sunday School Union, 1965), p. 97.

[38]Joel E. Spingarn Papers, Box 95-6; Freeman Henry Morris Murray Papers, Howard University: Moorland-Spingarn Research Center, Box 33.

[39]J. Max Barber, "The Niagara Movement at Harpers Ferry," The Voice of the Negro, 3, No. 10 (October, 1906), p. 408.

[40]W.E.B. DuBois, "A Word," In Reverdy C. Ransom's The Negro: The Hope or the Despair of Christianity (Boston: Ruth Hill Publisher, 1935), n.p.

[41]Reverdy C. Ransom, "The Spirit of John Brown,"

The Spirit of Freedom and Justice (Nashville: A.M.E.
Sunday School Union, 1926), pp. 22-23.

[42]Ransom, "William Lloyd Garrison," The Spirit of
Freedom and Justice, pp. 12-13.

[43]DuBois, Dusk of Dawn, pp. 88-92; Ransom,
Pilgrimage, p. 163.

[44]Ransom, Pilgrimage, p. 164; DuBois, Dusk of Dawn,
pp. 94-95; Elliott M. Rudwick, "The Niagara Movement,"
The Journal of Negro History, 12, No. 3, July 1957,
pp. 198-200. For more details on the relationship of
DuBois and Trotter, see Fox, The Guardian of Boston, pp.
101-14.

[45]Meier, Negro Thought in America, p. 182.

[46]Scheiner, Negro Mecca, pp. 200-01.

[47]Charles Flint Kellog, NAACP: A History of the
National Association for the Advancement of Colored
People, 1, 1909-1920 (Baltimore: John Hopkins Press,
1967): Langston Hughes, Fight for Freedom: The Study
of the NAACP (New York: Berkley Medallion Book, 1962,
pp. 16-24; Meier, Negro Thought in America, p. 182;
DuBois, Dusk of Dawn, p. 224. For a detailed exposition
on the relationship of Ida B. Wells and William Monroe
Trotter with the NAACP, see Duster, Crusade for Justice:
The Autobiography of Ida B. Wells, pp. 322-28, and Fox,
The Guardian of Boston, William Monroe Trotter, pp.
115-44.

[48]Ransom, The Spirit of Freedom and Justice, p. 45.

[49]Ransom, The Spirit of Freedom and Justice, p. 50.

[50]Charles V. Hamilton, The Black Experience in
American Politics (New York: Capricorn books, G.P.
Putnam's Sons, 1973), p. 250.

[51]For more extensive information on Ohio's key
black political figures, see David A. Gerber, Black Ohio
and the Color Line, 1860-1915, pp. 345-70; Russell H.
Davis, Memorable Negroes in Cleveland's Past (Cleveland:
The Western Reserve Historical Society, 1969), pp.
23-33; Kenneth L. Kusmer, Black Cleveland: The Making
of a Ghetto, 1870-1930, pp. 92-96, 113-14, 122-40.

[52]Ransom, The Spirit of Freedom and Justice, p. 152.

[53]Ransom, The Spirit of Freedom and Justice, p. 153.

[54]Ransom, The Spirit of Freedom and Justice, p. 150.

[55]Reverdy C. Ransom to George A. Myers, October 17, 1896, Box 2; George A. Myers Papers, Ohio Historical Society, Columbus Ohio.

[56]Felix James, "The Civic and Political Activities of George A. Myers," Journal of Negro History, 58, No. 2 (April, 1973), pp. 175-76.

[57]Ransom to Myers, October 17, 1896, Box 2; George A. Myers Papers, Ohio Historical Society.

[58]Indianapolis Freeman, September 16, 1896, December 12, 1896, January 2, 1897, January 9, 1907, January 16, 1897, January 23, 1897, January 30, 1897; The Cleveland Gazette, January 16, 1897, February 6, 1897.

[59]Indianapolis Freeman, December 12, 1896.

[60]Logan, The Betrayal of the Negro, p. 98; Burkett and Newman, Black Apostles, pp. 198-99; John P. Green, Fact Stranger Than Fiction, (Cleveland: Riehl Co., 1920), pp. 267-270.

[61]Leslie H. Fishel, Jr., "The Negro in Northern Politics, 1870-1900," Mississippi Valley Historical Review, 42 (December 1955) 466-89; Logan, The Betrayal of the Negro, p. 97.

[62]Fox, The Guardian of Boston, pp. 149-50.

[63]John Morton Blum, The Republican Roosevelt (New York: Atheneum, 1970), pp. 44-47; Harlan, Booker T. Washington, pp. 311-13.

[64]Fox, The Guardian of Boston, pp. 150-51; Meier, Negro Thought, p. 164.

[65]Fox, The Guardian of Boston, p. 152.

[66] Meier, _Negro Thought_, pp. 186-87.

[67] Ransom, _The Spirit of Freedom and Justice_, p. 60.

[68] Ransom, _The Spirit of Freedom and Justice_, pp. 60-61.

[69] DuBois, _Dusk of Dawn_, p. 235.

[70] DuBois, _Dusk of Dawn_, p. 233.

[71] Ransom, "Editorial, Hunting Big Game Out of Africa," _A.M.E. Review_, (October 1912), p. 140; Scheiner, _Negro Mecca_, pp. 205-6; DuBois, _Dusk of Dawn_, pp. 233-34.

[72] DuBois, _Dusk of Dawn_, pp. 234-35.

[73] _A.M.E. Review_, October 1912, pp. 118-24.

[74] Ransom, "Editorial, The Negro's Political Consciousness," _A.M.E. Review_ (July, 1912), pp. 84-85.

[75] Ransom, "Editorial, White Black Birds," _A.M.E. Review_ (January, 1913), p. 265.

[76] Alexander Walters, _My Life and Work_ (New York: Fleming H. Revell, 1917), p. 186.

[77] Alexander Walters, "The Aftermath," _A.M.E. Review_ (January, 1913), pp. 239-40.

[78] Arthur S. Link, _Woodrow Wilson and the Progressive Era, 1910-1917_ (New York: Harper Torchbooks, 1963), pp. 64-65.

[79] Walters, _My Life and Work_, pp. 195-96.

[80] Ransom, "Editorial, Segregation," _A.M.E. Review_ (January, 1913), pp. 229-30.

[81] Ransom, "Editorial, President Wilson, Trotter and the American People," _A.M.E. Review_ (January, 1915), pp. 309-18.

[82] Ransom, "Editorial, Woodrow Wilson," _A.M.E. Review_ (April, 1924), pp. 212, 213.

[83] DuBois, _Dusk of Dawn_, p. 237.

[84]DuBois, _Dusk of Dawn_, p. 237.

[85]Ransom, "Editorial, Republican Defeat," _A.M.E. Review_ (January, 1917), p. 164.

[86]_Crisis_, 15, No. 6 (April, 1918), p. 296.

[87]Ransom, "Seeking a Seat in Congress and a Voice in Government," _A.M.E. Review_ (April, 1918), pp. 228-31.

[88]Ransom, "Editorial, National Presidential Campaign," _A.M.E. Review_ (July, 1920), p. 38.

[89]Ransom, _Pilgrimage_, pp. 280-81.

[90]Ransom, "Why Vote for Roosevelt?" The _Crisis_, 39, No. 11 (November, 1932), p. 343.

[91]Davis, _Black Americans in Cleveland_, p. 277.

[92]Ransom, "The Negroes' Bewildering Political Predicament," p. 4, Ransom Papers, Wilberforce University Archives.

Summation and Conclusions

"With faith in ourselves and an
unfaltering trust in God, we
would resolve that while we were
once under the white man's feet
and for fifty years have bowed
before him in inferior ways, the
next fifty we will 'stand erect,
neither below or beneath, but by
the side our white fellow
citizens'."[1]

How shall we assess the life and contribution of Reverdy Cassius Ransom, variously referred to by historians August Meier, June Sochen, And Richard Bardolph, as a "militant radical orator," black social Gospel Minister," and "yet another of the giants of the Negro vanguard?"[2] Perhaps the reflections of preacher and theologian, Howard Thurman, offer some illumination of that assessment:

> It is difficult to identify precisely the influences that shape and fashion the life of an individual. The enigma is the process at work in the private world of an individual that finds its expression in the thoughts, words, and actions that ultimately emerge. It has been aptly said that the time and place of a man's life is the time and place of his body, but the meaning and significance of a man's life is as creative, as vast, and as far-reaching as his gifts, his dreams, and his response to his times can make them.[3]

This was certainly true of Reverdy C. Ransom.

Born black into a world where he was neither slave nor free, Ransom's childhood, youth, and young adulthood occurred during a time when black people experienced both the optimism of Reconstruction and the pessimism of the "nadir." He spent his entire career fighting for black rights, whether as a member of the Afro-American Council, the Niagara Movement, the Constitution League, the NAACP, or the Republican or Democratice parties. Primarily, however, Ransom worked for racial advancement through the black church, and thus it is significant that the Social Gospel Movement was emerging as a potent force in American Protestant Christianity when he began his ministry. Subsequently, he pastored in many cities where the problems Social Gospelers worked to address were most blatant and while pastoring in Chicago, Ransom developed both intellectual and personal friendships with prominent Social Gospel leaders. While the realities of race and the rise of the Social Gospel provide the backdrop for Ransom's actions and involvements, they do not completely answer the question of who he was and why he responded as he did to those realities.

Ransom was born fatherless and more significantly,

164

poor. The poverty of his first thirty or more years undoubtedly contributed to his sensitivity and sympathy to the problems and pains of the poor and oppressed. Those early economic hardships, especially those associated with his employment and that of his mother, predisposed Ransom to become a strong advocate for the rights of laboring people everywhere. His later espousal of Christian Socialism is an indiction of the persistent and evolving commitment to the welfare of working persons.

Reared in a household with many other children for a period of his life, Ransom, as the lone child of his mother, was rejected by the other siblings, an experience reflected later in his identification with the "outsiders" of the society. His reflection upon Jesus' ministry to the prostitutes and sinners would confirm him in the rightness of this identification. The state of Ohio offered Blacks few opportunities during Ransom's youth, as his experience with segregated education attests. Perhaps as a result of the discrimination to which he was exposed, Ransom was opposed to distinctions on grounds of race in any form. He considered "Jim Crowism" to be not only antithetical to democracy, but an affront to God, the Creator of all. He received his religious precepts and his basic sense of self-work from his mother.

The dominant influence in Ransom's early life was Harriet Ransom. Hers was the most powerful and sustaining influence during his formative years and was reflected in his life-long quest for excellence, a standard upon which she insisted. That black and white were equal before God was a conviction that Harriet Ransom held onto tenaciously. She believed God, in creating her son, had bestowed upon him intelligence and ability equal to that of her white employers' sons. And of equal significance to Ransom was his mother's insistence that a lack of education and ignorance was responsible for the lowly plight of black people.

Other persons, such as Daniel A. Payne and Benjamin Arnett affected Ransom's growth and development over the years and were conspicuous in their support of him at crucial periods in his life. The religious and intellectual nurture of the A.M.E. Church and Wilberforce University and the teachings about God's relationship to black people were important influences as well. Reverdy knew that he was Harriet's son, but

165

more importantly he believed that he was created by God. The patrimonial concern of God for black people was the centerpiece of Ransom's thought and action. God was a God of justice as well as a God of mercy and love.

Ransom was made aware of his own frailties and weaknesses through his swearing, card-playing, and pilfering as a youth and his short-lived early marriage which subsequently ended in divorce. He was characteristically unself-righteous when the shortcomings of other human beings were brought into question. Later in his ministry, he would seek to prod the church into becoming an inclusive community in which everyone would be welcome without regard to their economic, political, social or moral circumstances.

It is clear that Ransom's identification with those who had periodically "fallen from grace" emanated from his personal experience. He not only acknowledged the dissolution of his first marriage and his refusal to expel from one of his early pastorates a single woman who became pregnant, but admitted his long-time problem with alcoholism as well.[4] Thus, Ransom was considered by many who knew him as either a saint or a sinner, and since very few people were neutral when it came to estimating his character, he was either fiercely loved or fiercely hated. Some of his church opponents considered him a tough political in-fighter who never failed "to punish an enemy." Nearing the end of his long life, Ransom responded to such charges with "I have never concealed anything I have ever done. I will tell you, or them, anything they want to know about me or my life. Let them judge."[5] The following critique shall be based upon Ransom's thought and action within the context of his times.

Ransom came to maturity during the "Age of Progress." The concept of progress, according to theologian Martin E. Mary, "implied a dynamic view of history, full of development and change."[6] According to its proponents, there was an inevitability about progress, and mankind was moving inexorably "onward and upward." Most Americans and many Social Gospelers accepted the doctrine of progress, linking it as they did to the on-going development and expansion of white Anglo-Saxon civilization around the world. Some Social Gospelers like Josiah Strong asserted that the Anglo-Saxon race was destined by its superior racial endowments to rule the world, bringing Christian

166

civilization to its backward peoples. Ransom also believed in progress, but his faith in it differed drastically from Strong's position as the following statement indicates:

> The forces of the world are in alignment
> to evolve from the doctrine of race and
> color into the doctrine of man. If the
> white man seeks to build his supremacy
> on the foundations of the doctrine of
> race and color, then by the doctrine of
> race he shall be overthrown.[7]

Ransom spoke those words as a black Christian heavily influenced by the progressive and essentially optimistic Social Gospel, but also as a black American experiencing the demeaning realities of racial proscription. Thus, Ransom's optimism was tempered by this nation's continued refusal to accept black people as equals. The "problem of racial and cutural contacts."[8] within the United States prevented Ransom, like DuBois, from completely accepting the Social Gospel's faith in progress. This was the paradox of Ransom's life, for as a believer in the oneness of the human race, he was constantly confronted with the reality of oppression based upon race. In his efforts to counter the racism of white Christians, Ransom came perilously close to promulgating yet another theory based on the questionable assumption that black people's racial endowments predisposed them to a spiritual superiority lacking in white people.

Like most of his Social Gospel contemporaries, Ransom also tended to equate America and her ideals with the eventual emergence of the Kingdom of God. This conviction that the United States by Divine Providence had been chosen for a unique mission in the world dated back to the seventeenth century Puritans' concept of the Holy Commonwealth and the concept of Manifest Destiny promulgated periodically during much of the nineteenth century. When tied to imperialism and the idea of progress, as invariably occurred, the idea that America and Western civilization were duty-bound to Christianize the world caused the pernicious coupling of the flag and the cross. Ransom criticized American Christianity for its acquiescence in and basic support of the country's imperialism toward the colored nations of the world. He accepted the view that America had a mission to the world, but contended that the mission was to bring into being a world of brotherhood, justice and love rather than a world of domination, subjugation, and colonialism. He believed that the foundation for that new world of justice was the unrealized ideals embodied in the Declaration of Independence, the Constitution and the Emancipation Proclamation. Ransom's rejection of America's foreign policy excursions seems to have been based exclusively upon the country's brutal and unjust treatment of black people. He came to believe that because America had forfeited its mission of universal fraternity, black people became the only bona fide Christians capable of bringing about the Kingdom of interracial brotherhood.

Ransom's way of rationalizing the hyprocrisy of the white Christians was to argue that black people had inherited the burden of their righteous responsibility. Thus did he reformulate an unquestionably racist theory. Even while accepting the fact that the purpose of Ransom's racialist Christianity was the construction of a truly interracial and just world, one must note the racist assumptions from which the theory emerged.[9]

Indeed, Ransom must also be judged in light of his basic acceptance of the racialist theories of his day. It is true that Ransom rejected the prevailing Social Darwinist notion that certain races were genetically inferior and predestined to servitude and control by superior races. He responded with the argument most often used to counter Social Darwinism: the assertion that environment, not heredity (is) responsible for the conditions of peoples and nations. Even so, Ransom accepted and believed that particular peoples and nations were genetically endowed with special characteristics and traits. In fact, his idea of the peculiar mission of black people to the world was inextricably tied to his understanding of their natural musical talent, eloquence of speech, friendliness, deep emotional endowment, and their unique spiritual nature. There is an obvious contradiction here. Ransom attacked one set of genetic theories while promulgating yet another set based upon the nebulous postulation that racial groups possessed certain in-born characteristics and traits. There is doubt that he recognized the contradiction.

Despite such blatant theoretical blind spots, Ransom's overall church theory and practice demonstrated many strengths. He had the foresight to grasp the powerful effect urbanization and black migration would have upon the black church. Secondly, he anticipated a growing social clevage between the relatively more prosperous and educated northern Blacks and the poor, basically uneducated southern black migrant. Ransom primarily applied Social Gospel theory to address these concerns. Thirdly, he understood that the problems and prospects emanating from urbanization could not be adequately addressed by the local church, but required the concerted actions of entire religious denominations.

As an urban pastor, Ransom appropriated for his own purposes various Social Gospel auxiliaries, including the United Society of Christian Endeavor and the Epworth League, and in his capacity as denominational leader and editor, he urged the consolidation of small urban churches, the establishment of designated city missions funded by denominational resources, and encouraged A.M.E. seminaries to develop their curricula offerings to reflect the urban reality. Furthermore, and most importantly, Ransom formed the Institutional Church and Social Settlement in 1900 as his model of an urban twentieth century church. Its numerous programs for youth and adults - day care for working mothers, employment bureau, manual training department, and physical fitness programs - were among other attempts to meet the needs of urban dwellers. Institutional Church also afforded Ransom an opportunity to bridge the widening gap between those who had eminence and social staus and those who did not. Ransom appealed to black elites who had rejected the old-time religion and who were attracted by Institutional's social betterment programs and its nondenominationalism. Ransom'a appeal to poor Blacks was based upon the social services provided them by Institutional Church and its willingness to accept them whatever their circumstances.

Thus, Ransom's response to the Social Gospel was the direct result of his pastoral experiences beginning in Allegheny City (1888). The circumstances under which his parishioners lived revealed to him the need for a broader conception of society if their needs were to be met. Ransom was greatly attracted to the Social Gospel by its contention that the church was in the world to change society. It is crucial to recognize, however, that identification with the Social Gospel is closely related to his understanding of the religious heritage of black people and his understanding of the black church. Influenced by their experience with God as

creator, sustainer and liberator, Blacks saw the hand of
God in their deliverance from slavery. Consequently,
they believed that His Presence continued with them on
their journey to full equality. The church was central
to the realization of that racial hope, being God's
earthly institution.

The day of brotherhood was assured as long as God
and man worked toward its fulfillment.[10] It is
difficult to gauge whether Ransom's exposure to the
Social Gospel or his understanding of the black church
most influenced the scope and direction of his ministry.
It is evident that both supported his activist image of
the church. Consistent with that image, Ransom
exemplified in his ministry the clergyman as social and
political activist. Thus, his activities within the
Niagara Movement and other protest organizations, his
founding of the Institutional Church and Social
Settlement and the Fraternal Council of Negro Churches,
his twelve-year tenure as editor of the A.M.E. Review,
and even his life-long preoccupation with politics, must
be recognized as the conscious involvements of a
Christian activist seeking to implement his vision of a
racially just society. It is significant that Ransom
often used the terms black church, black people, and
black community interchangeably. Such usage may
indicate a fuzziness of terms, but I think not. Rather,
it seems to illustrate the breadth and inclusiveness of
Ransom's vision for the black community. His concern
was to broaden the basis of race unity to the extent
that good and bad, virtuous and vicious, rich and poor,
educated and ignorant, and the vulgar and the refined
could join together for the good of the race and of the
nation. Although seemingly paradoxical, when Ransom
urged racial solidarity, he desired that Blacks use
their unified power to bring about a truly interracial
society. Ransom, not unlike other Social Gospelers,
believed the assertion that all men are created equal,
and that the equalitarian concept offered the world a
new understanding of humanity. He did not doubt that
God had ordained America's democratic institutions, but
he vigorously rejected the contention that God had
ordained America's treatment of black people. He never
relented in his opposition to America's racial bias, and
his life-long commitment to racial justice is evident in
a letter written by Ransom in 1951 at the age of ninety
to the National Council of the Arts, defending DuBois
from McCarthyite attacks:

...I have known Dr. DuBois more than fifty years, ever since he graduated from Harvard University. I have worked with him in organizations and committees, fighting for justice, freedom and equality for almost two generations...For over fifty years, Dr. DuBois has stood for the things for which George Washington fought, that Thomas Jefferson wrote in the Declaration of Independence, and the guarantees contained in the Constitution of the United States. Millions of Americans of African descent thou(gh) inarticulate, aspire to achieve the things advocated by Dr. DuBois; namely, full and complete integration into every phase of American life on the basis of absolute equality...If this case comes to trial, will they try to end this man's brilliant career by placing on him a martyr's crown? In case they do it would be the most powerful blow for Negro freedom and equality...We are not turning back a single inch. Americans of African descent are on the march for freedom against segregation, proscription...denial, and every influence that would prevent them from obtaining their goal of complete freedom and equality as American citizens...Millions of us here have courage without fear, and shall firmly stand to support the foundations upon which this nation was established, and upon which it stands today. It remains the brightest hope for all Americans, regardless of race, creed, or color. If we could ascend from the depths of slavery from whence we came to the place we occupy today, we can also achieve the goals of brotherhood and peace for which we strive.[11]

This letter is an appropriate valedictory for one who fought relentlessly for social and racial justice. A reviewer of Ransom's biography wrote of his life, "...(It) has been a strong pilgrimage, full of struggle and achievement. This pilgrimage has been well worth taking. With all its faults, it is a life worth living."[12]

Footnotes

[1] Ransom, "Editorial, The New Emanicipation," A.M.E. Review (January, 1913), p. 264.

[2] Meier, Negro Thought, p. 221; Sochen, The Unbridgeable Gap, p. 15; Bardolph, Negro Vanguard, p. 145.

[3] Howard Thurman, ed., A Track to the Water's Edge: The Olive Schreiner Reader (New York: Harper & Row Publishers, 1973), pp. xviii-xix.

[4] Ransom, Pilgrimage, pp. 48-50.

[5] The Cleveland Call and Post, June 25, 1955, n.p. Ransom Papers, Wilberforce University.

[6] Marty, Righteous Empire, p. 189.

[7] Ransom, "Editorial, For Black and White, Not Things Equal and Separate, But the Same Things, Review (October, 1915), pp. 351-52.

[8] DuBois, Dusk of Dawn, pp. 25-26.

[9] Fullinwinder, The Mind and Mood of Black America, p. 45.

[10] Smith, "Slave and Theology...," Church History, Vol. 41 (December, 1972), pp. 497-512.

[11] Ransom to the National Council of the Arts, Sciences and Professions, October 26, 1951. W.E.B. DuBois Papers, University of Massachusetts. For additional information regarding the McCarthy period, see Philip S. Foner, The Voice of Black America (New York: Simon and Schuster, 1972), pp. 865-66; Walls, A.M.E.Z. Church, pp. 525-26.

[12] J. Wilfred Holmes, Pittsburgh Courier, March 5, 1950.

APPENDIX A

Crossing the Color Line

by

Reverdy C. Ransom

The American Color Line is neither geographical, geometrical, nor, like the Mason and Dixon line, sectional. It winds its serpentine course in and out, through every phase of American life. Race prejudice and race antagonism are by no means confined to the United States, but this country is preeminent in the ignoble distinction it has achieved in the matter of treating a fellow human being on the basis of the color of his skin. The chief causes that have divided men throughout the ages have been religion, language, nationality.

Not even the so-called pagan nations of antiquity erected a line of division between men, based on the complexion of the skin. Those who go back to Cain in an effort to account for the origin of black peoples, do not well, for the weight of the evidence presented by science is strongly in favor of the contention that the first human dwellers on this planet were not white men. This being true, it follows that whatever else it may have been, the mark upon Cain was not a black mark.

A woman, Miriam, the sister of Moses, was the first person on record to draw the color line, by objecting to her brother's black wife. On this matter Jehovah made his attitude quite clear by smiting Miriam with leprosy.

The separateness of the Jews and the Samaritans was not based upon color. The almost universal race antipathy to the Jew is not due to the color of his skin but to his aloofness, religion, customs.

American color prejudice outstrips the worst forms of religious fanaticism in its arrogance, blindness, cruelty and injustice. It has refused to be convinced by logic, won by kindness, softened by religion, or restrained by law. It answers all argument, and repels every friendly overture, by withdrawing behind the impassible barrier of a white skin. Before this, reason must be silent and justice impotent.

173

From many different angles of advantage, attempts have been made to cross the color line. After the abolition of slavery, it was said by the best friends the Negro ever had, with his citizenship and the right to vote he would be able to protect himself from re-enslavement, to maintain in his rights and to take any place in the life of the nation which, according to the standards of ability and worth, was accorded to others. But by the evasiveness of the Supreme Court, the acquiescence of the North and the intimidation, violence, the nullification of the Constitution by legal subterfuge in the South, the mantle of his citizenship has been so rent and torn that it cannot cover his political nakedness.

Again the Negro was told, if he could but lift the dense cloud of ignorance that overhung his race, intelligence and education would remove his chief handicap. According to the census of 1900, the Negro had reduced his illiteracy 52 1/2 percent in forty years. It is confidently predicted that the census of 1910 will show that 68 percent of our Negro population are at least able to read and write. There is less illiteracy among the Negroes of the United States than is to be found in several European powers of the first and second class. The Negro has not only acquired an elementary education, but in high schools, colleges and universities, in competition with white boys and girls, he has demonstrated his intellectual equality in every branch of knowledge, in many cases taking the highest honors. If it is asserted that these were "picked Negroes," we have but to reply that their competitors were the picked white youth of the nation. When the Negro approaches the color line armed with intelligence and a first-class education, he is repulsed with the charge that his education was all wrong. It tends to make him "dissatisfied," "unwilling to work," "puts notions in his head," and "makes him aspire to get out of his proper place."

Again, the Negro was told, if he would eschew politics, cease agitating for his rights, refrain from protesting and complaining against restrictions placed upon him, and devote himself to industry, through an industrial education in agriculture and the trades, he would be able to allay prejudice against him on account of color, because of his usefulness to the community in which he might reside. Dr. Booker T. Washington, himself a Negro, is the chief apostle of this doctrine.

174

The sentiment of the South accepts it; the philanthropy of the North supports it. Its Negro propagator is free to speak in those sections of the South where color prejudice is most pronounced and virulent; he is honored in the highest seats of learning and received in the most exclusive circles of society. But the supposed beneficiaries of this propaganda find that the color line which nullified the right to vote and refused to accept as a passport a high school or college diploma, is quite as inflexible and unyielding in the presence of a hoe, a plow, a saw, a hammer, a chisel or a trowel, however skillfully wielded. The labor unions continue to discriminate against Negroes, and in those states where they are the most numerous there exist laws which prevent them moving from place to place except under hard conditions. In these states laws have been passed which impose a penalty of $500 and imprisonment upon any emigrant agent who tries to induce immigration not only from the state, but to different countries of the same state.

The possession of money is a pass-word which, in America, is supposed to cause all doors to open. The Negro has been assured that is was not his color, but his poverty that caused the color line to be so rididly drawn against him. If he became a land owner, had a bank account, engaged in business, etc., men would treat with him without regard to his color. Dr. Booker T. Washington is authority for the statement (The Story of the Negro, Vol. II, P. 47) that "the Negro farmers in 1909 owned, in the Southern States, not less than thirty thousand square miles of land. This is an amount of territory nearly equal to five New England States: Vermont, New Hamphsire, Massachusetts, Connecticut and Rhode Island." He estimates that the Negroes in the United States own at the present time not less than $500,000,000 worth of taxable property. There are at the present time, 47 banks operated and controlled by Negroes in this country.

Now, a Negro may have a diploma from Harvard or Yale, possess an unblemished character and be worth $100,000, only to find that because of his character, education and wealth, the color line was a more impassable barrier to him than to some poor uneducated Negro who did not try to get "out of his place."

A sense of political, civil and social justice has caused this country to accord to the Negro a place which makes his position unique among this race throughout the world. This is the only country where the Negro and the white man dwell together upon terms of equality before the law. It is true that there are many Negroes living under the English, French and German flags, but these Negroes do not live in England, Germany of France, but in colonies ruled by them beyond the seas or in islands in the midst of the sea. The Negroes of Bermuda or Martinique create no race friction in England or France. But American color prejudice is like the trail of a serpent. Now that many Negroes have both the means the leisure for foreign travel, they find both in England and on the continent, that at hotels, on public carriers, in theatres, or even in society, are they anywhere treated in a manner to remind them of their color,--except some American objects to their presence.

Admittedly, democracy is one of the great problems that has been given to America to solve, not only for herself, but to demonstrate for the emulation of mankind. Not that white men shall prove their ability to perpetuate self-government for and by themselves. They have the greater problem, the greater ever undertaken by mankind - to join with men of an entirely opposite variety of the human race, by living and cooperating with them on terms of absolute political, civic and industrial equality and justice.

This is the very heart of the Christianity which America professes for herself and would extend to the ends of the earth; it is the spirit of her Declaration of Independence; it is the written word of her Constitution which is the supreme law of the land. If America fails of her opportunity by treating men according to their wealth instead of their worth, their color instead of their character, their race instead of their rights, then we must confess the failure of both her Democracy and Christianity and await the rise of a new civilization above the ruins of her shattered hopes and broken pledges to mankind.

An overruling majority of the people on the earth are colored and not white. The attitude of natural inferiority and general contempt with which the black people in particular and the darker races in general have been regarded by the white peoples, begins to show signs of a change. Commercial considerations may have more weight in bringing it about than either ethical, religious or political influences. Japan, with the

176

white man's rifle in her hands, has already crossed the color line. China has begun to stir, India is growing restless, light is breaking over the Dark Continent. Trade relations cannot be friendly, nor great and profitable markets established with the dark-skinned people in whose faces the color line is continually flaunted with contempt.

"The Universal Races' Congress," called to meet in London next July, marks the beginning of a better era. Here men of the white, the black, and darker peoples of mankind will meet to exchange opinions, learn each other's point of view and frankly discuss points of difference, in an effort to arrive at a better understanding. Diversity of color should not make for division among men, any more than it does among birds, or beasts or flowers; it is rather the keynote of unity, of harmony.

Now in another form, let the old question come: How hardly shall a black man cross the color line? Once let him be recognized as a brother and a man, and then all things will be possible. The ethiopian will have no need to try to change his skin as he walks without let or hindrance in the paths of men.

Lynching and American Public Opinion

by

Reverdy C. Ransom

When Truth desired a hearing and Liberty a voice, men have in the past looked to Faneuil Hall. These walls have been articulate with the cry of the oppressed, not only of our country, but throughout the world. No spot on earth is more sacred to the cause of freedom and justice than the ground upon which we stand. while one stone rises above another here, Faneuil Hall will remain a standing challenge to tyrants and tyranny. By the high ideals it has championed, Faneuil Hall doctrine has done more than any other to make this country's history worth recording. The acts of Faneuil Hall audiences have done more to influence American public opinion in the right direction than have the acts of Congress.

With the flight of years a great transformation has been wrought in public sentiment and the personnel of the audiences assembled here. In the old days white audiences thronged these walls to hear white men, representing the best heart and brain of the nation, plead for liberty and justice for the poor oppressed blacks. Today the burden rests upon black men and women to come here and appeal to a public opinion and a public press, which is, for the most part, indifferent or hostile. Our appeal is for the supremacy of civilization over barbarism and savagery.

We are here not in the spirit of anger or that discouragement which has abandoned hope. We are here not so much to denounce and assail, as to appeal to this nation to forsake its sins, to cast off its bloody robes of murder, to throw back into the deepest abysmal pit of hell its lyncher's torch and seek that righteousness that exalteth a nation.

The question that confronts us is older than the Declaration of Independence, the Magna Charta, or the laws of Moses upon the tables of stone; it goes back to the time when God beheld the blood of Abel caying from the ground. Can this nation, consecrated to freedom, afford to face the future with the mark of Cain branded upon its brow?

Lynching, which is fast becoming a national crime, reaches far beyond the helpless victim who perishes horribly by the fury of the mob. The question that most vitally concerns us is not one of race antipathy or sympathy; it concerns our Christianity, democracy and civilization itself. Some who object to protests of this kind tell us to make our people cease committing crimes against women, and then lynching will cease. But in eighty percent of the lynchings this crime is not even alleged.

In approaching a question like that of the freedom with which Negroes may be put to death by mobs, we should seek for causes. We have not far to seek. Primarily, it sprang out of the desire of the former slave-holding states to repress the Negro. The South, in order to justify itself in these barbarities, began by blackening his character, by painting him as a monster who menaced the safety of women. By continually dinning this into the ears of this country and of the world, they have finally so quieted the public conscience that now a Negro charged with any crime, and sometimes with no crime at all, may be lynched with impunity anywhere in the South and occasionally in the North. The conscience of the nation has become so seared that it is no longer horrified when in the state of Pennsylvania or Georgia a human being is burned to death at the stake. The newspaper press does not use its powerful influence to arouse public opinion against the iniquity, while the pulpit, which should be the first to lead in an attempt to purge the nation of this foul blot, is, for the most part, silent.

Negroes themselves are largely to blame for the contempt in which they are held and the impunity with which their liberties and their lives may be invaded. Sheriffs, mayors, courts, governors, will not take seriously into account the interest of a people who have lost or surrendered the right to retaliate or call them to account at the ballot box. Mobs do not quail when there is no fear that their wild brutalities will be answered by a volley of bullets.

I am unwillingly, but slowly, coming to the conclusion that the only way for the Negro in particular, and the dark-skinned peoples in general, to win and hold the respect of white people is to mete out

179

to them a white man's measure in all the relations of
life.

In at least seven of the states of this Union the
Negro holds the balance of political power. He should
use this weapon in an effort to stir the national
government against lynching. We are all familiar with
lynching in the Southern States. The national
government can do anything it desires to do when the
public welfare or interests demand it. The national
government found a way to interfere when the boll weevil
was destroying the cotton crop in Texas and other
southern states. The national government found a way to
legislate on the quesiton of marriage in relation to the
Mormon Church, and would immediately take steps to
nullify any action the State of Utah might take on this
subject contrary to the prevailing public opinion.

Are not the rights of human beings as sacred as the
cotton crop? Is not the doctrine of the inviolability
of human life more sacred than this nations' attitude
toward the doctrine of the Mormon Church?

But the action of this government in abrogating the
treaty with Russia furnishes a still more striking
example as to how the lynching evil can be combatted.
The treaty was abrogated because American citizens of
the Jewish race visiting in Russia did not receive the
same treatment accorded to other American citizens.
Now, the treaty of the United States with Great Britain
contains the clause "the most favored nation."

We would advise that Negro subjects of the British
Empire who come to this country numerously from the
British West Indies travel freely throughout the
Southern States and when they are Jim Crowed and
otherwise assaulted and degraded, that they appeal to
the British Government on the ground that their treaty
rights have been violated. Let them urge that England
abrogate its treaty with the United States, unless the
government of the United States guarantees to British
subjects of the Negro race the same treatment as is
accorded to other subjects.

Why were American public opinion and American
statesmen aroused to such a height of indignation on
behalf of the Jew? Is it because they are in love with
the Jews, or rather is it because of the Jewish vote?
One of the reasons why the Negro's cause in this country

180

has in recent years sadly gone from bad to worse is because misguided Negro leaders have counseled them to an attitude of submission, which is both unmanly and un-American. He has largely lost or surrendered his right to vote to the nulification of the Fifteenth Amendment.

To demand the enforcement of the Fifteenth Amendment today is to be branded as "an enemy of both races," "a fanatic," "a mischievous agitator." To all outside inteference the South says: "Leave the Negro to us, we understand him, and know best how to deal with him both for his own good and the welfare of the South." President Taft, who had boldly committed himself to the doctrine of race discrimination, pipes his grand diapason in harmony with this sentiment by declaring, that the Negro "ought to come and is coming more and more under the guardship of the South!"

With far more justification, we reply on behalf of the Negro--Leave the Southern white people to us. We have lived among them for two and a half centuries, we both know and understand them. We have nursed their children, built their homes, and for more than two hundred years we have fed and clothed them. When they took up arms to destroy the Union in order to bind us in perpetual chains, we did not fire their cities with the torch, nor rise in violence against them, but protected their property, their helpless women and children. Leave them to us. We have imbibed not the ideals of feudalism, but of democracy; we are Americans filled with the spirit of the twentieth century. Leave them to us, and we will make the free public school universal throughout the South and open alike to all, without regard to race, creed or color. We will make free speech as safe in Mississippi as it is in Massachusetts; we will abolish lynching and usher in a reign of law, of courts and juries, instead of the shot gun, the faggot and the mob. We will abolish peonage, elevate and protect labor and make capital secure. Leave them to us; our chivalry shall know no color line, but our womanhood shall be protected and defended, and our citizens, regardless of race or color, shall be permitted to particiapte in the government under which we live. Leave them to us, and we will make them know their place and keep it, under the Consitution as amended. We will remove the last vestige of Jim Crowism under the forms of law, and make the places of public necessity, convenience, recreation and amusement, open alike to all without respect to race or color. We will make intelligence, character and worth, instead of race and color, the sole test of recognition and preferment for all. Thus as North and South divided over the Negro, so would the Negro unite them in the only bond of union that can stand the test of time-fraternity, justice and righteousness.

Bibliography

Abell, Aaron I. <u>The Urban Impact on American Protestantism 1865-1900</u>. Cambridge: Harvard University Press, 1943.

Allen, Frederick Lewis. <u>The Big Charge: America Transforms Itself 1900-1950</u>. New York: Harper & Brothers, 1952.

_____. <u>Only Yesterday</u>. New York: Harper, 1957.

Allen, Robert L. <u>Reluctant Reformers: Racism and Social Reform Movements in the United States</u>. New York: Anchor Books, 1975.

Ahlstrom, Sidney E. <u>A Religious History of the American People</u>. Volume 2. New York: Image Books, 1975.

Anderson, Jervis, ed. <u>A. Philip Randolph: A Biographical Portrait</u>. New York: Harcourt Brace Jovanovich, Inc., 1972.

Aptheker, Herbert, ed. <u>A Documentary History of the Negro People in the United States. Volume 1 & 2</u>. Secaucus, New Jersey: The Citadel Press, 1951.

_____, ed. <u>W.E.B. DuBois: The Education of Black People</u>. Amherst: University of Massachusetts Press, 1973.

_____, ed. <u>The Correspondence of W.E.B. DuBois 1868-1963</u>. Amherst: University of Massachusetts Press, 1973.

Arnett, Benjamin W. <u>The Budget of the A.M.E. Church</u>. Dayton, Ohio: Christian Pubishing House, 1881-84.

_____ and Mitchell, S.T. <u>Wilberforce Alumnal</u>. Xenia, Ohio: The Gazette Printing Co., 1885.

Averill, Lloyd James. <u>American Theology in the Liberal Tradition</u>. Philadelphia: Westminister Press, 1967.

Bancroft, Edgar A. <u>Doctor Gunsaulus, the Citizen</u>. Chicago: ?, 1921.

Bardolph, Richard, <u>The Negro Vanguard</u>. New York: Vintage

Books, 1961.

Barnett-Wells, Ida B. "Rev. R. C. Ransom, B.D." A.M.E. Recorder 47 (January 25, 1900).

Bell, Derrick A., Jr. Race, Racism and American Law. Boston: Little, Brown & Co., 1973.

Berlin, Ira. Slaves Without Masters: The Free Negro in the Antebellum South. New York: Vintage Books, 1976.

Bernard, Jessie L. Marriage and Family Among Negroes. Englewood Cliffs, N.J.: Prentice Hall, Inc., 1966.

Berry, Llewellyn L. A Century of Missions of the A.M.E. Church 1840-1940. New York: Gutenberg Printing Co., 1942.

Berwanger, Eugene H. The Frontier Against Slavery. Urbana: University of Illinois Press, 1967.

Blackwell, James E. and Janovitz, Morris. Black Sociologists: Historical and Contemporary Perspectives. Chicago: The University of Chicago Press, 1974.

Bigglestone, W. E. "Oberlin College and the Negro Student, 1865-1940." Journal of Negro History 86, No. 3 (July, 1971): 198-219.

Bliss, William A. P. The Encyclopedia of Social Reform. New York: Funk & Wagnalls Co., 1897.

Blockson, Charles L. Pennsylvania's Black History. Philadelphia: Portfolio Associates, Inc., 1975.

Blum, John Morton. The Republican Roosevelt. New York: Atheneum, 1970.

Bond, Horace Mann. Black American Scholars--A Study of Their Beginnings. Detroit: Balcamp Publishing, 1972.

Bontemps, Arna, ed. American Negro Poetry. New York: Hill and Wang, 1963.

Bouleware, Marcus H. The Oratory of Negro Leaders: 1900-1968. Westport, Conn.: Negro Universities

Press, 1969.

Brauer, Jerald C. <u>Protestantism in America: A Narrative History</u>, Revised ed. Philadelphia: The Westminister Press, 1965.

Broderick, Francis L. <u>W.E.B. DuBois: Negro Leader in a Time of Crisis</u>. Stanford, California: Stanford University Press, 1959.

Brotz, Howard, ed. <u>Negro Social and Political Thought 1850-1920</u>. New York: Basic Books, Inc., 1966.

Brown, John G. "Wilberforce University: Twenty-Third Commencement Exercises - A Brilliant Closing." <u>A.M.E. Recorder</u> 24 (July 8, 1886).

Brown, Hallie Q. <u>Pen Pictures of Pioneers of Wilberforce</u>. Xenia, Ohio: Aldine Press, 1937.

Brown, Sterling. <u>The Negro Caravan</u>. New York: The Dryden Press, 1941.

Bucke, Emory J. <u>The History of American Methodism</u> 2. New York: Abingdon Press, 1964.

Buckler, Helen. <u>Doctor Dan: Pioneer in American Surgery</u>. Boston: Little Brown & Co., 1954.

Bullock, Henry A. <u>A History of Negro Education in the South; from 1619 to the Present</u>. New York: Praeger Publishers, 1970.

Burkett, Randall K. and Newman, Richard, eds. <u>Black Apostles: Afro-American Clergy Confront the Twentieth Century</u>. Boston: G.K. Hall & Co., 1978.

Butcher, Charles S. "A Historical Study of Efforts to Secure Church Union Among Independent Negro Methodists." B.D. Thesis, Howard University School of Religion, 1939.

Cantor, Milton, ed. <u>Black Labor in America</u>. Westport, Conn.: Negro Universities Press, 1969.

Carey, John J. "The Intellectual World of Carlyle Marney." <u>The Bulletin</u> 4, No. 1 (March, 1980) 1-6.

Carter, Purvis M. "The Astigmatism of the Social Gospel

185

1877-1901." M.A. Thesis, Howard University, 1950

Coleman, Lucretia H. Poor Ben: A Story of Real Life. Nashville: A.M.E. Sunday School Union, 1890.

Coan, Josephus R. Daniel Alexander Payne: Christian Educator. Philadelphia: A.M.E. Book Concern, 1935.

Cushman, Robert E. Leading Constitutional Decisions. New York: F.S. Crofts & Co., 1940.

Daniels, John. In Freedoms' Birthplace: A Study of the Boston Negro. Boston: Houghton Mifflin Co., 1914.

Davis, Arthur P. From the Dark Tower: Afro-American Writers 1900 to 1960. Washington, D.C.: Howard University Press, 1974.

Davis, Russell H. Black Americans in Cleveland: From George Peake to Carl B. Stokes 1796-1969. Washington, D.C.: The Associated Publishers, Inc., 1972.

_____. Memorable Negroes in Cleveland's Past. Cleveland: Western Reserve Historical Society, 1969.

Delaney, Martin R. The Condition, Elevation, Emigration and Destiny of the Colored People of the United States. Philadelphia: Published by the author, 1852; reprint ed., New York: Arno Press, 1968.

Detweiler, Frederick G. The Negro Press in the United States. Chicago: The University of Chicago Press, 1922.

Drake, St. Clair. "Churches and Voluntary Associations in the Chicago Negro Community." Report of the Official Project 463-54-3-386, Works Progress Administration (Chicago, 1940).

DuBois, W.E.B. The Philadelphia Negro: A Social Study. Philadelphia: University of Pennsylvania, 1899; reprint ed., New York: Schocken Books, 1967.

_____. The Souls of Black Folk. New York: A. C. McClure, 1903; reprint ed., Greenwich, Conn.: Fawcett Premier Book, 1961.

186

_____. Dusk of Dawn: An Essay Toward An Autobiography of a Race Concept. New York: Harcourt, Brace & World, Inc., 1940; reprint ed., New York: Schocken Books, 1968.

_____, ed., Atlanta University Publication No. 8, Vol. 2. Atlanta: Atlanta University Press, 1903' reprint ed., New York: Octagon Books, Inc. 1968.

Dunbar, Alice M. Masterpieces of Negro Eloquence. New York: The Bookery Publishing Company, 1914.

Duster, Alfreda M., ed. Crusade for Justice: The Autobiography of Ida B. Wells. Chicago: The University of Chicago Press, 1970.

Ferris, William H. The African Abroad or His Evolution in Western Civilization, Vol. 2. New Haven: The Tuttle and Taylor Press, 1913.

Ferry, Henry J. "Francis J. Grimke: Portait of a Black Puritan." Ph.D. dissertation, Yale University, 1970.

Fishel, Leslie H., Jr. "The Negro in Northern Politics 1870-1900." Mississippii Valley Historical Review 42 (December, 1955) 466-89.

Foner, Philip S. Organized Labor and the Black Worker 1619-1973. New York: International Publishers, 1974.

_____. The Voice of Black America. New York: Simon & Schuster, 1972.

_____. American Socialism and Black Americans: From the Age of Jackson to World War II. Westport Conn.: Greenwood Press, 1977.

Fox, Stephen R. The Guardian of Boston: William Monroe Trotter. New York: Atheneum, 1970.

Franklin, John Hope. From Slavery to Freedom: A History of Negro Americans, 3rd edition. New York: Vintage Books, 1969.

Frazier, E. Franklin. The Negro in the United States. New York: MacMillan Co., 1949.

_____. The Negro Family in the United States, revised ed. Chicago: University of Chicago, Press, 1966.

Frederickson, George M. The Black Image in the White Mind: The Debate on Afro-American Character and Destiny 1817-1914. New York: Harper Torch Books, 1971.

Fullwinder, S.P. The Mind and Mood of Black America. Homewood, Ill.: The Dorsey Press, 1969.

Galbreath, Charles B. History of Ohio. New York: The American Historical Society, Inc. 1925.

Garraty, John A. Interpreting American History: Conversations with Historians, Part II. New York: The MacMillan Company, 1970.

Gatewood, Willard B. Black American and the White Man's Burden 1893-1903. Urbana: University of Illinois Press, 1975.

George, Carol V. R. Segregated Sabbaths: Richard Allen and the Rise of Independent Black Churches, 1816-1840. New York: Oxford University Press, 1973.

Gerber, David A. Black Ohio and the Color Line 1860-1915. Chicago: University of Illinois Press, 1976.

Gossett, Thomas F. Race: The History of an Idea in America. New York: Schocken Books, 1965.

Green, John P. Fact Stranger than Fiction. Cleveland: Riehl Co., 1920.

Handy, Robert T. A Christian America: Protestant Hopes and Historical Realities. New York: Oxford Univeristy Press, 1971.

Hamilton, Charles V. The Black Experience in American Politics. New York: G. P. Putnam's Sons, 1973.

Hanson, J. W., ed. The World's Congress of Religions. Chicago: International Publishing Co., 1894.

Harlan, Louis R. Booker T. Washington: The Making of a Black Leader, 1856-1901. New York: Oxford

188

University Press, 1972.

_____, and Smock, Raymond W., ed. The Booker T. Washington Papers, Volume 5, 1899-1900. Chicago: University of Illinois Press, 1976.

Haynes, George E. The Negro at Work in New York City. New York: Columbia University, Longman & Green Co., 1912; reprint ed., New York: Arno Press, 1968.

Henderson, Thomas W. "Manager's Weekly Letter: A Visit to Chicago." A.M.E. Recorder 47 (March 15, 1900).

Henri, Florette. Black Migration: Movement North, 1900-1920. New York: Anchor Books, 1976.

Hickock, Charles T. "The Negro in Ohio 1802-1870." Ph.D. dissertation. Western Reserve University, 1896.

Higham, John. Strangers in the Land; Patterns of American Nativism 1860-1925. New York: Atheneum, 1963.

Hofstader, Richard. Social Darwinism in American Thought, revised edition. Boston: Beacon Press, 1955.

_____. The Age of Reform: From Bryan to F.D.R. New York: Vintage Books, 1955.

_____, ed. The Progressive Movement 1900-1915. Englewood Cliffs, N.J.: Prentice-Hall, Inc., 1963.

Hopkins, Charles H. The Rise of the Social Gospel in American Protestantism 1865-1915. New Haven: Yale University Press, 1940.

_____, White, Ronald C., eds. The Social Gospel: Religion in Changing America. Philadelphia: Temple University Press, 1976.

Hudson, Winthrop S. Religion in America: An Historical Account of the Development of American Religious Life, 2nd ed. New York: Charles Scribner's Sons, 1973.

Hughes, Langston. Flight for Freedom: The Story of the NAACP. New York: Berkley Medallion Books, 1962.

_____. Selected Poems. New York: Alfred A. Knopf, 1965.

James, Felix. "The Civic and Political Activities of George A. Myers." Journal of Negro History 58, No. 2 (April, 1973) 166-78.

James, Janet W. Women in American Religion. Philadelphia: University of Pennsylvania Press, 1980.

Johnson, James Weldon. Along This Way: The Autobiography of James Weldon Johnson. New York; The Viking Press, 1968.

_____. The Book of Negro Poetry, revised ed. New York: Harcourt Brace & World, 1959.

_____. Black Manhattan. New York: Atheneum, 1969.

Jordan, Winthrop. White Over Black American Attitudes Toward the Negro 1550-1812. Baltimore: Penguin Books, Inc., 1968.

Kellogg, Charles F. NAACP: A History of the National Association for the Advancement of Colored People, 1909-1920. Baltimore: Johns Hopkins Press, 1967.

Killian, Charles D. "Bishop Daniel A. Payne: Black Spokesman for Reform." Ph.D. dissertation, Indiana University, 1971.

_____, ed. Sermons and Addressed 1853-1891 by Bishop Daniel A. Payne. New York: Arno Press, 1972.

Kusmer, Kenneth L. Black Cleveland: A Ghetto Takes Shape, 1890-1915. Urbana: University of Illinois Press, 1976.

Lee, Benjamin F. Sketch of Wilberforce University. Xenia, Ohio: Torchlight Printing Co., 1884.

Leuchtenburg, William E. The Perils of Prosperity 1914-32. The University of Chicago Press, 1958.

Link, Arthur S. Woodrow Wilson and the Progressive Era 1910-1917. New York: Harper Torchbooks, 1963.

Linn, James W. Jane Addms: A Biography. New York: D. Appleton-Century Company, 1935.

Litwak, Leon F. North of Slavery: The Negro in the Free States 1790-1860. Chicago: The University of Chicago Press, 1961.

Lloyd, Henry D. Mazzini and other Essays. New York: G.P. Putnam's Sons, 1910.

Logan, Rayford W. The Betrayal of the Negro: From Rutherford B. Hayes to Woodrow Wilson. London: Collier Books, 1965.

_____, ed. W.E.B. DuBois: A Profile. New York: Hill & Wang, 1971.

Lynch, Hollis R. Edward Wilmot Blyden: Pan-Negro Patriot, 1832-1912. New York: Oxford University Press, 1967.

Marty, Martin E. Righteous Empire: The Protestant Experience in America. New York: The Dial Press, 1970.

May, Henry F. Protestant Churches and Industrial America. New York: Harper & Brothers Publishers, 1949.

Mazzini, Joseph. The Duties of Man and other essays. New York: E. P. Dutton & Co., 1915.

McGinnis, Frederick A. A. History and an Interpretation of Wilberforce University. Blanchester, Ohio: Brown Publishing Co., 1941.

_____.The Education of the Negro in Ohio. Blanchester, Ohio: Curless Publishing Co., 1962.

Meier, August. Negro Thought in America 1880-1915: Racial Ideologies in the Age of Booker T. Washington. Ann Arbor, Mich.: Ann Arbor Paperbacks, 1966.

_____, Rudwick, Elliott M., eds. From Plantation to Ghetto: An Interpretative History of American Negroes. New York: Hill and Wang, 1966.

Miller, Kelly. Radicals & Conservatives and other Essays

on the Negro In America. New York: Schocken Books, 1968; reprint of 1908 work entitled Race Adjustment.

Morgan H. Wayne, ed. American Socialism 1900-1960. Englewood Cliffs, N.J.: Prentice-Hall, Inc. 1965.

Nash, Gary B., Weiss, Richard, eds. The Great Fear: Race in the Mind of America. New York: Rinehart & Winston, Inc., 1970.

Nielson, David G. Black Ethos: Northern Urban Negro Life and Thought, 1890-1930. Westport, Conn.: Greenwood Press, 1977.

Newton, Joseph Fort. Some living Masters of the Pulpit, studies in religious personality. New York: George H. Doran Co., 1923.

O'Neil, William L. The Progressive Years: America Comes of Age. New York: Dodd, Mead & Company, 1975.

Osofsky, Gilbert. Harlem: The Making of a Ghetto, 1890-1930, 2nd ed. New York: Harper Torchbooks, 1971.

Ovington, Mary White. The Walls Came Tumbling Down: The Autobiography of Mary White Ovington. New York: Schocken Books, 1970.

Payne, Daniel A. Recollections of Seventy Years. New York: Arno Press and the New York Times, 1969.

_____. History of the A.M.E. Church. ed., Smith, C. S. Nasville: A.M.E. Sunday School Union, 1891.

Perlman, Daniel. "Stirring the White Conscience: The Life of George Edmund Haynes." Ph.D. dissertation. New York University, 1972.

Quarles, Benjamin. The Negro in the Making of America. New York: Collier Books, 1964.

Raboteau, Albert J. Slave Religion: The "Invisible Institution" in the Antebellum South. New York: Oxford University Press, 1978.

Ransom, Emma S. "The Home-Made Girl." A Speech delivered to the Convention of the Northeastern Federation of

Women's Clubs, Boston, Massachusetts, 1905. Ransom
Papers, Payne Theological Seminary.

Ransom, Reverdy C. "Too Cultured for His Flock."
Christian Recorder 24 (November 18, 1886).

_____. "Annual Conference" Christian Recorder 26
(September 27, 1888).

_____. "Dr. C. S. Smith's Version of the
Apostles Creed." A.M.E. Recorder 27 (April 24,
1890).

_____. "Why This Haste," Christian Recorder 28
(August 28, 1890).

_____. "Chicago Paragraph." Christian Recorder
47 (July 6, 1899).

_____. "The Institutional Church and Social
Settlement." Christian Recorder 48 (November 29,
1900).

_____. "The Institutional Church." Christian
Recorder 48 (March 7, 1901).

_____. " A Christmas Meditation." undated.
Wilberforce University Archives, Wilberforce, Ohio.

_____. School Days at Wilberforce. Springfield,
Ohio: The New Era Co., 1892.

_____. Disadvantages and Opportunities of Negro
Youth. Cleveland: Thomas & Mattell, 1894.

_____. "Out of the Midnight Sky." A Thanksgiving
Address delivered at Mt. Zion Congregational
Church, Cleveland, Ohio, November 30, 1893.
Wilberforce University Archives, Wilberforce, Ohio.

_____. " The Negro and Socialism." 13 A.M.E.
Review (October, 1896) 192-200.

_____. "The Industrial and Social Conditions of
the Negro." A Thanksgiving Sermon delivered at
Bethel A.M.E. Church, Chicago, November 26, 1896.
Wilberforce University Archives, Wilberforce, Ohio.

_____. Deborah and Jael: A Sermon delivered to

the Ida B. Wells Women's Club at Bethel A.M.E. Church, Chicago. (Chicago: Chrystal Print, n.d.) Payne Seminary Archives, Wilberforce, Ohio.

_____. "A Programme for the Negro." A.M.E. Review 16 (April, 1900) 423-30.

_____. "The First Quadrennial Report of the Institutional Church and Social Settlement." Presented at the 22nd General Conference, A.M.E. Church, Chicago, May, 1904. Wilberforce University Archives, Wilberforce, Ohio.

_____. "Duty and Destiny." A Thanksgiving address deliverd at Bethel A.M.E. Church, November 24, 1904. Wilberforce University Archives, Wilberforce, Ohio.

_____. Smith, C.S.; Hawkins, J.R., eds. The A.M.E. Church Yearbook, 1917-18; Hawkins, J.R., Hunt, J. eds. The A.M.E. Church Yearbook, 1922-23.

_____. The Spirit of Freedom and Justice: Orations and Speeches. Nashville: A.M.E. Sunday School Union, 1926.

_____. "Why Vote for Roosevelt?" Crisis 39, No. 11 (November, 1932) 343-44.

_____. "The Negroes' Bewildering Political Predicament." An address delivered at Douglas High School, Cleveland, Ohio, November 3, 1934. Wilberforce University Archives, Wilberforce, Ohio.

_____. The Negro: The Hope or the Despair of Christianity. Boston: Ruth Hill Publisher, 1935.

_____, ed. The Yearbook of Negro Churches, 1935-36; 1939-40. Philadelphia:A.M.E. Book Concern.

_____. Preface to the History of the A.M.E. Church. Nashville: A.M.E. Sunday School Union, 1950.

_____. The Autobiography of Harriet Ransom's Son. Nashville; A.M.E. Sunday School Union, 195?

_____. "Confessions of a Bishop." Ebony 5

(March, 1950) 72-80.

_____, ed. The Glow of Promethean Fire over the Marching Negro Race by Karol Marcinkowski. Published at Wilberforce University, 1950.

Raper, Arthur. The Tragedy of Lynching. Chapel Hill: The University of North Carolina Press, 1933; reprint ed., New York: The American Library, Inc., 1969.

Redkey, Edwin. Black Exodus: Black Nationalist and Back-to Africa Movements, 1890-1910. New Haven: Yale University Press, 1969.

Reimers, David M. Protestantism and the Negro. New York: Oxford University Press, 1965.

Resak, Carl, ed. The Progressives. New York: Bobbs-Merrill, 1967.

Reuter, Edward B. "The Mulatto in the United States." Ph.D. dissertation, University of Chicago, 1918; reprint ed., New York: Negro Universities Press, 1969.

Rhys, Ernest, ed. Essays: The Duties of Man and other Essays by Joseph Mazzini. New York: E.P. Dutton & Co., 1936.

Rosenberg, Louis J. Mazzini: the prophet of the religion of humanity. Chicago: C. H. Kerr & Co., 1903.

Ross, B. Joyce. J.E. Spingarn and the Rise of the NAACP 1911-1939. New York: Atheneum, 1972.

Rudwick, Elliott M. "The Niagara Movement." The Journal of Negro Histoy 42, No. 3 (July, 1957) 177-200.

_____. W.E.B. DuBois: Propagandist of the Negro Protest. New York: Atheneum, 1969.

Scheiner, Seth. Negro Mecca: A History of the Negro in New York City 1865-1920. New York: New York University Press, 1965.

Silone, Ignazio. The Living Thoughts of Mazzini. New York: Longmans, Green & Co., 1939.

Singleton, George A. The Romance of African Methodism:

A Study of the African Methodist Episcopal Church.
New York: Exposition Press, 1952.

Simmons, William J. Men of Mark: Eminent, Progressive
and Rising. New York: George M. Revell & Co., 1887;
reprint ed., Chicago: Johnson Publishing Company,
Inc., 1970.

Sinkler, George. The Racial Attitudes of American
Presidents: From Abraham Lincoln to Theodore
Roosevelt. Garden City, N.Y.: Doubleday & Comapny,
Inc. 1971.

Smith, Amanda. An Autobiography of Mrs. Amanda Smith,
The Colored Evangelist. Chicago: Meyer and Brothers
Publishers, 1893.

Shade, William G., Herrenkohl, Roy C., eds. Seven on
Black: Reflections on the Negro Experience in
America. Philadelphia: J. B. Lippincott Comapny,
1969.

Smith, Charles S. A History of the African Methodist
Episcopal Church 2 Philadelphia: A.M.E. Book
Concern, 1972.

Smith, Edwin P. The Golden Stool. London: Holborn
Publishing House, 1927.

Smith, Timothy L. "Slavery and Theology: The Emergence
of Black Christian Consciousness in Nineteenth
Century America." Church History 41 (December,
1972) 497-512.

Snider, Wayne L. Guernsey County's Black Pioneers,
Patriots and Persons. Columbus: Ohio Historical
Society, 1979.

Sochen, June. The Unbridgeable Gap: Blacks and Their
Quest for the American Dream 1900-1930. Chicago:
Rand McNally & Co., 1972.

Spear, Allan H. Black Chicago: The Making of a Negro
Ghetto 1890-1920. Chicago: The University of
Chicago Press, 1967.

Spencer, Samuel R., Jr. Booker T. Washington and the
Negro's Place in American Life. Boston: Little,
Brown and Company, 1955.

196

Stampp, Kenneth M. The Era of Reconstruction 1865-1877. New York: Vintage Books, 1965.

Steward, Theophilus G. Fifty Years In the Gospel Ministry. Philadelphia: A.M.E. Book Concern, 1914.

Stokes, Arthur P. "Daniel Alexander Payne: Churchman and Educator." Ph.D. dissertation, Ohio State University, 1973.

Stone, Irving. Clarence Darrow for the Defense. Garden City, N.Y.: Doubleday & Co., 1941.

Talbert, Horace. Sons of Allen: Together with a Sketch of the Rise and Progress of Wilberforce University. Xenia, Ohio: Aldine press, 1906.

Taylor, Graham. Religion in Social Action. New York: Dodd & Mead Co., 1913.

_____. Pioneering on Social Frontiers. Chicago: University of Chicago Press, 1930.

_____. Chicago Commons Through Forty Years. Chicago: Chicago Commons Association, 1936.

Terrell, Mary Church. A Colored Woman in a White World. Washington, D.C.: National Association of Colored Women's Clubs, Inc., 1968.

Thornbrough, Emma Lou. "The National Afro-American League 1887-1908." Journal of Southern History 27, No. 4 (November, 1961) 494-512.

Thurman, Howard. The Negro Spiritual Speaks of Life and Death. New York: Harper & Brothers, 1947.

_____, ed. A Track to the Water's Edge: The Olive Schreiner Reader. New York: Harper & Row Publishers, 1973.

Ullman, Victor. Martin Delaney: The Beginnings of Black Nationalism. Boston: Beacon Press, 1971.

United States Bureau of the Census. Negro Population 1790-1915. New York: The New York Times, 1968.

United States Bureau of the Census. Ohio 1860.

197

Wade, Louise C. Graham Taylor: Pioneer for Social
     Justice, 1851-1938. Chicago: University of Chicago
     Press, 1964.

Wagner, Jean. Black Poets of the United States: From
     Paul Lawrence Dunbar to Langston Hughes. Translated
     by Kenneth Doublas. Chicago: University of Illinois
     Press, 1973.

Walls, William J. History of the African Methodist
     Episcopal Zion Church: Reality of the Black Church.
     Charlotte, N.C.: A.M.E.Z. Publishing House, 1974.

Washington, Booker T.; DuBois, W.E.B.; Chestnutt, C.W.;
     Smith, W.H.; Keeling H.T.; Dunbar, P.L.; and
     Fortune, T.T. The Negro Problem. New York: Arno
     Press and the New York Times, 1969.

Weisenberger, Francis P. "William Sanders Scarborough:
     Early Life and Years at Wilberforce." Ohio History
     71, No. 3 (October, 1962) 203-26.

Weiss, Nancy J. The National Urban League 1910-1940. New
     York: Oxford University Press, 1974.

Williams, Walter L. "Ethnic Relations of African
     Students in the United States with Black Americans.
     Journal of Negro History 65 (Summer, 1980) 228-49.

Wilmore, Gayraud S. Black Religion and Black Radicalism:
     An Examination of the Black Experience in Religion.
     Garden City, N.Y.: Anchor Books, 1973.

Wills, David. "Aspects of Social Thought in the African
     Methodist Episcopal Church, 1884-1910." Ph.D.
     dissertation, Harvard University, 1975.

_____. "The Meaning of Racial Justice and the
     Limits of American Liberalism." The Journal of
     Religious Ethics, Vol. 6/2 (Fall, 1978) 199-215.

_____. "Reverdy C. Ransom: The Making of an
     A.M.E. Bishop." Burkett & Newman, eds; Black
     Apostles: Afro-American Clergy Confront the
     Twentieth Century. Boston: G. K. Hall, 1978.

Woodson, Carter G. A Century of Negro Migration.
     Washington, D.C.: Association for the Study of
     Negro Life and History, 1918.

_____. *The Education of the Negro Prior to 1861.* New York: G. P. Putnam's Sons, 1915.

_____. *The History of the Negro Church.* Washington, D.C.: The Associated Publishers, Inc., 1921.

_____. *Negro Orators and Their Orations.* Washington, D.C.: The Associated Publishers, Inc., 1925.

Woodward, C. Vann. *Origins of the New South 1877-1913.* Baton Rouge: Louisiana State University Press, 1951.

_____. *The Burden of Southern History.* New York: Vintage Books, 1960.

_____. *The Strange Career of Jim Crow*, 2nd rev. ed. New York: Oxford University Press, 1966.

Wright, Richard R., Jr. *The Negro in Pennsylvania: A Study in Economic History.* Philadelphia: A.M.E. Book Concern, 1912; reprint ed., Arno Press and the New York Times, 1969.

_____. *The Bishops of the African Methodist Episcopal Church.* Nashville: A.M.E. Sunday School Union, 1963.

_____. *87 Years Behind the Black Curtain: An Autobiography.* Nashville: A.M.E. Sunday School Union, 1965.

DOCUMENTS

Minutes of the Fifty-fifth Ohio Annual Conference of the
    A.M.E. Church (1885).

Minutes of the Eighteenth Pittsburgh Annual Conference
    of the A.M.E. Church (1885).

Minutes of the Fifty-Sixth Ohio Annual Conference of the
    A.M.E. Church (1886).

Minutes of the Twentieth Pittsburgh Annual Conference of
    the A.M.E. Church (1887).

Minutes of the Twenty-First Pittsburgh Annual Conference
    of the A.M.E. Church (1888).

Minutes of the Twenty-Third Pittsburgh Annual Conference
    of the A.M.E. Church (1890).

Minutes of the Fourteenth Iowa Annual Conference of the
    A.M.E. Church (1896).

Minutes of the Fifteenth Iowa Annual Conference of the
    A.M.E. Church (1897).

Minutes of the Sixteenth Iowa Annual Conference of the
    A.M.E. Church (1898).

Minutes of the Seventeenth Iowa Annual Conference of the
    A.M.E. Church (1899).

Minutes of the Twenty-Second Quadrennial Conference of
    the A.M.E. Chuch (1904).

Minutes of the Ninety-Seventh New York Annual Conference
    of the A.M.E. Church (1912).

Minutes of the Twenty-Fourth Quadrennial Conference of
    the A.M.E.Church (1912).

Minutes of the Twenty-Seventh Quadrennial Conference of
    the A.M.E. Church (1924).

PRIVATE DOCUMENTS

Wilberforce   University   Biennial   Catalogue,   1883.
    Wilberforce University Archives.

Wilberforce   University Catalogue, 1884-85. Wilberforce
    University Archives.

Faculty   Minutes,   Wilberforce   University   1885-90.
    Wilberforce University Archives.

The   Wilberforce   University   Alumnal, 1894. Wilberforce
    University Archives.

Ninth   Quadrennial   Report   of   Wilberforce   University,
    1900. Wilberforce University Archives.

Dedication Souvenir, St. James A.M.E. Church. Cleveland,
    Ohio, 1953. Wilberforce University Archives.

Catalogue,   Oberlin   College,   1882-83. W.E. Biggleston,
    Archivist,   Oberlin   College   to   Calvin S. Morris,
    January 29, 1980.

201

PERSONAL CORRESPONDENCE

Claude   A. Barnett Papers, Chicago   Historical Society.

Charles   W.   Chestnutt   Papers,   Fisk   University.

W.E.B.   DuBois   Papers,   University   of   Massachusetts.

Joseph B. Foraker Papers, Cincinnati Historical Society.

Freeman Henry Morris Murray Papers, Moorland-Spingarn
    Research Center, Howard University.

George   A. Myers Papers, Ohio Historical Society, Inc.

Reverdy   C. Ransom   Papers, Wilberforce   University
    Archives.

Reverdy C. Ransom Papers, Payne Theolgical Seminary

Arthur   Spingarn   Papers, Moorland-Spingard   Research
    Center, Howard University.

Joel E. Spingarn Papers, Moorland-Spingarn Research
    Center, Howard University.

Daniel Hale Williams Collection,   Moorland-Spingarn
    Research Center, Howard University.

Interview: Calvin S. Morris, Mrs. Myrtle Teal Ransom,
    September 23, 1979, Tawawa Chimney Corner,
    Wilberforce, Ohio.

NEWSPAPERS AND MAGAZINES

A.M.E. Christian Recorder, 1886, 1890, 1897-99, 1901.

A.M.E. Church Review, 1886, 1889, 1897, 1901, 1905, 1910, 1912-24.

Baltimore Afro-American, 1959.

Chicago Evening Post, 1903.

Chicago Inter-Ocean, 1899, 1900.

Chicago Journal, 1899.

Chicago-Record Herald, 1903.

Chicago Tribune, 1903.

Cleveland Call and Post, 1955-56.

Cleveland Gazette, 1893, 1894, 1896-97.

Crisis, 1918, 1932.

Ebony, 1950.

Indianapolis Freeman, 1896-97.

Literay Digest, 1903.

New York Amsterdam News, 1959.

Pittsburg Courier, 1950.

Time, 1950.

Voice of the Negro, 1906.

Washington Bee, 1903.